I0815408

Praise for *Be Your Own Bestie*

"Truly inspiring and hilarious, this book is the bestie you need to build the best bestie in you. A beautiful work that can be beautifully applied to your life by way of practical advice and soothing affirmations. We need more of this bestie energy everywhere!"

— **Margaret Cho**, actress and comedian

BE YOUR OWN BESTIE

BE YOUR OWN BESTIE

A No-Nonsense Guide to Changing the Way You Treat Yourself

MISHA BROWN

HAY HOUSE LLC
Carlsbad, California • New York City
London • Sydney • New Delhi

Published in the United States by: Hay House LLC, www.hayhouse.com®
P.O. Box 5100, Carlsbad, CA, 92018-5100

Cover and interior design: Lisa Vega

Cataloging-in-Publication Data is on file at the Library of Congress

Hardcover ISBN: 978-1-4019-9830-1
E-book ISBN: 978-1-4019-9831-8
Audiobook ISBN: 978-1-4019-9832-5

6th Printing

Printed in the United States of America

This product uses responsibly sourced papers, including recycled materials and materials from other controlled sources.

The authorized representative in the EU for product safety and compliance is Penguin Random House Ireland, Morrison Chambers, 32 Nassau Street, Dublin D02 YH68, Ireland. https://eu-contact.penguin.ie

For the women who shaped me:
To my Nana, who loved me without limits and
taught me that true acceptance
has no conditions.

To my Grandma Brown, who gave me
the gift of stories and a love for books that shaped
the way I see the world.

And to my mom, my biggest supporter, whose
unwavering belief in me made
me believe in myself.

This book is a piece of me,
and I am because of you.

CONTENTS

INTRODUCTION

Hey, Bestie! If we've already met, welcome! Seriously, I'm so glad you joined me here. And if you're new to the Bestiehood: Hi, I'm Misha! You might know me from social media, where I've spent the past several years bringing the sass and snark, calling out bad behavior, and—most importantly—supporting my Besties. In this time, my followers have become my friends, and we've been through it all together: laughing as I put bullies in their place, connecting through stories of the shit we all have to deal with, and even grieving through the loss of loved ones.

Both online and in my real life, most of my besties are women. I have felt so taken care of, uplifted by, and cheered on by the women in my life, and I have such a deep appreciation and love for them. This has also given me a front-row seat to their struggles with all of the Chads, the insane demands on them to be perfect moms, boss babes, and not age a day in the process. The lived experience of women so often goes unnoticed or underappreciated, and I'm here to say: *I see you, girl.*

That's why I'm writing this book. Because I see you. I've seen you up close. Like in the real-life pits of motherhood, marriage, and work where you are just trying your best to keep it together.

My friend Nicole was just like you. For years, she had been doing everything she could to keep her relationship intact. She'd vent to me on the phone, hiding in her bathroom, where I could hear the baby crying as her husband sat out in the living room like raising a kid just wasn't his department. Just like the laundry, the meals, the doctors' appointments, even the goddamn balloons for their baby's birthday party.

One night, while she was sobbing on my shoulder, I said something that just kind of came out. "Imagine you're in a little rowboat. Not a cruise ship, not a yacht, just a worn little thing barely big enough for you. But you've got your husband in there. And your baby. And the dog. And every time someone in that boat gets tired of paddling, you pick up their oar. He stops trying? You paddle harder. He complains the ride's not smooth enough? You adjust course, even if it's directly into a storm he fucking created. He wants to stretch out? You curl yourself up to make him more comfortable. And anytime the boat starts to tip, you don't say a word. You just scoop out the water with your hands, smiling like nothing's happening."

I looked into her tired eyes and said, "Because after all, you packed a life jacket for him. You made sure he had what he needed. But you don't have one for yourself. Because you figured you could just hold on a little bit longer. You really didn't think you deserved one. You told yourself if you just love hard enough, sacrifice enough, prove your worth enough, that maybe he'll start rowing again."

I let that hang in the air between us for a second.

"But love isn't supposed to make you drown."

And that's when she broke. Because somewhere along the way, Nicole had forgotten that she even had the right to be in the boat.

Listen, Bestie, it's okay to want to be loved, to be needed, to be chosen. But not at the cost of going under. And especially not if you're the one keeping the whole damn boat afloat. And this is a lesson that took time for me to learn myself.

I've always been the bestie who will hold your hand and say, "Okay, bitch, it's time to get back up!" But I wasn't always that kind and supportive to myself. Not knowing how to care for myself in this way led me to terrible relationships, unfulfilled dreams, and becoming an alcoholic.

This book is called *Be Your Own Bestie*, which is actually quite serendipitous since it is something I said to myself to kick-start my own self-love journey, and it also just so happens to share the acronym for the common alcohol-related phrase of "bring your own bottle."

Something you should know about me: I am totally a type A personality. I map out pretty much anything I can. And my journey into relearning how to even like myself, let alone love myself, was no different.

The core idea for this book began when one day, after waking up hugging the minibar in a bleak hotel room, I sat down and wrote out how I wanted to spend the next year, which was the goal I set for how long I wanted to commit to this new me. I thought about negative words other people and my own self had used in the past to describe me, and if I could figure out a creative way to reclaim them. Eventually I landed on the word *sassy*. And with that I came up with my guide—the S.A.S.S. method. I decided I would use this guide to intentionally show up for myself as my own best friend.

S.A.S.S. stands for:

— **S**elf-Reflection Is a Bitch

— **A**ffirm the Shit Out of Yourself

— **S**tand Your Ground

— **S**culpt the Life You Want

Over the course of the past six years, I have come back to and followed this simple series of steps anytime I feel like some aspect of my life can be improved. It's a way to get down to the root of what's not working and how I can change that to live my best, fullest life; it helps me understand why I feel the way I do at any given moment and how I got there. It's a way of packing up the negative stuff in my life, slapping a return label on it, and returning that shit to sender.

It's no mistake that, over the past six years, I've become the person my past self always wanted to be. And it all comes down to S.A.S.S., which I'm so excited to share with you, because you deserve to be the version of yourself that you love best and to surround yourself with the people who are reflective and supportive of the confidence and self-love you need to live your best life.

If you're a seasoned Bestie, you know I'm not in the business of bullshitting. And if you're a new Bestie-to-be, you'll soon learn that I don't offer glittery, empty platitudes that ignore the fact that this shit is hard to do in practice. S.A.S.S. might be fairly straightforward (and we're definitely going to have fun going through it together), but that doesn't mean the work it requires you to do won't be challenging at times.

Get ready to dig deep and get really honest with yourself. Each of us is accountable for our own change, and you are going to earn every drop of wisdom and insight S.A.S.S. will lead you to. You will need to own up to your mistakes, take the time to focus on yourself, and put up boundaries when necessary—and none of that is easy. If it were, there would be no reason to read this book. And there also wouldn't be any room to grow. So, when the going gets tough, when you find yourself questioning whether or not you can navigate this terrain, remember this: I promise you that the work is worth it. And I would never, ever lie to a bestie.

Now, that's not to say that everything that isn't working in your life at this moment comes down to you and only you; the world is *some* of the problem. When so much is being asked of you and you're racing around to do it all on a daily basis—to be a gold-star partner, parent, entrepreneur, or employee of the month, and so much more—how is it that you still feel left behind? Don't worry, we'll tackle that as well.

Making the choice to be my own bestie has been, hands down, the best decision I've ever made. It's offered me clarity about who I am, where I've been, where I'm going, and who I want to come along with me. I've learned to love and take care of myself in ways I didn't know were possible. And you can have all of this too, as we hold hands and skip down the yellow brick road toward the Emerald City (which, for our purposes, represents true happiness).

Whatever your dream is, whether it's writing a *New York Times* bestseller or just actually liking yourself, I am your sassy gay best friend who is going to grab you by your metaphorical ponytail and drag you toward getting there together. Lovingly, of course. You don't have to be the best version of yourself, the boss babe, or a perfectly curated version of you right now. You don't have to fit into your jeans from college, run the PTA, or perfect your sourdough recipe. You just have to be you. This book is designed for who you are right now, and I hope it will serve as a manual and support system to lead you to who you want to be in the future.

No matter how you feel as we start this journey together, you have the capacity to begin showing up for yourself in the way you deserve, Bestie. And I'll help you get there.

—Part I—

SELF-REFLECTION IS A BITCH

I really wish I could tell you that becoming your own best friend starts with bubble baths or plastering affirmations to your bathroom mirror and treating yourself to a pint of ice cream. Sorry, babe; that's like slapping a Band-Aid on an arm that just got chopped off. No, what you need to do is actually look into that bathroom mirror and ask yourself: *How the fuck did I get here?* And, also no, this isn't a cute, singular rom-com moment that will magically fix everything. Self-reflection is that girl who makes you sit in your own mess and look at it instead of convincing you that it's just a phase and you'll get over it soon.

But here's some good news. Once you face it, you can fix it! We all have baggage, some of it handed to us, and some of it that we've packed with our own choices. Maybe you grew up being told you weren't enough. Maybe you put up walls so high that no one could get over them, not even to love you. Maybe, like me, you handed over the reins of your life to people who didn't deserve to steer. Whatever it is, let's unpack that suitcase.

This section is about doing the messy, oftentimes uncomfortable work of self-reflection so you can take some accountability and stop being your own worst enemy. I'll share how I faced the harsh truth about my life, how my friend learned to let go of her mother's voice in her head, and how a co-worker's tough exterior was really just a defense mechanism. Most importantly, you'll learn to stop waiting for someone else to treat you like you're special and start doing it for your own damn self!

This might sting a little, but trust me, it's the first step to treating yourself like the best friend you've always needed. It won't be all bad. I'll throw in some jokes and feel-good moments, because laughter is definitely the best medicine. You've got this.

CHAPTER 1

HOW THE FUCK DID I GET HERE?

How the fuck did I get here? This single thought snapped me out of an 18-year delusion that I was a happy person who had his shit together and opened my eyes to the reality that I was living in a three-star hotel room in New Jersey. I had a view of the New York City skyline, the place where I had planned to fulfill my dreams of being on Broadway. But it was a place that was currently on the other side of the Hudson River—so close to everything I had dreamed, yet so, so far away.

I looked at the cigarette butts swimming in a disposable coffee cup I had turned into a makeshift ashtray, the empty pack of Camel Lights next to it, and the dozen or so empty beer cans that had been crushed and scattered around the room. And then I started to cry, because I am an emotional bitch, but also because I was suddenly acutely aware that my reality looked nothing like what I'd planned for or promised to myself.

As I spiraled—ahem, I mean reflected—on where things had gone off-course, I could suddenly see all the times life had gotten in the way of my dreams of making it big, deterring my goals of earning a career under the bright lights. And by life getting in the way, I mean that sometimes I made dumb decisions. Recently, I'd made a lot of them. Too many of those dumb decisions over the past decade had been because of [insert puking noise here] men. Bestie, I know, I *know*!

I cried for my unfulfilled potential, I cried for how sick I felt from the remarkable amount of alcohol I had consumed in the last few weeks, and I cried over my latest failed relationship.

Then after I cried so much I could have won a battle against the best waterproof mascara on the market, I started asking myself: *Why?* Why am I wearing the same fucking dirty sweatpants I've been wearing for weeks? Why am I still choosing relationships that I know aren't fair to me when I've already been taught this lesson repeatedly? Why have I not auditioned for a Broadway show in years when I keep telling myself that's what the goal is?

That night I went to bed with what felt like two opposing forces battling it out in my head. One was telling me that I was on the precipice of changing my life, and the other was saying I was foolish for believing I had any chance of changing who I was.

Hey, Bestie! You know, life is often like a messy-ass room. The longer you go without cleaning it, the messier your space becomes, and the more daunting it is to tidy it up.

You are not weak or stupid or unworthy because life has been life-y. You are not alone, and you are definitely not too far gone. But the better you're able to identify where life has hit you and knocked you off-course, the better you will be able to get en route and kick life right back in the balls by going after what you want anyway.

While I have all the confidence that you will take the reins of your life back, it will take work. Looking back isn't as easy as looking forward. Most people can tell you what they want out of life and where they want to go, but the real work begins with figuring out what has stopped you from getting there. Maybe you want to be more confident but you grew up with parents who were better at criticizing you than building you up. Maybe you want to figure out who you are but you're a single parent who spends most of your time focused on your children's needs. Maybe you are finally tired of keeping your emotions to yourself but you've been in a series of relationships where your feelings were constantly bulldozed over, like an old man pushing past you to get to the buffet.

This is simply your chance to take a breath, look around you, and say, "Wait a damn minute, how did it get this messy?"

I don't know about you, but I often get overwhelmed with the thought of tidying up an entire room, so I just start avoiding it altogether—except maybe to continue adding to the mess. But what if you stopped looking at the entire overwhelming room and instead just focused on picking up your clothes? Then maybe put some trash in the bin. Before you know it, you've made your bed, vacuumed, opened the window to air it out (you stinky bitch!) and *voila*! The room is clean.

That's going to be the goal here, and you're going to do it by breaking down your *whys* to make it all feel a lot more manageable. No matter where you find yourself in life right now, this is your starting point. And reflecting on how you got here, to this exact moment, can help you get where you want to go a lot faster. For me, once I stopped for a moment and really looked at how I came to find myself in that New Jersey hotel room that stunk of stale beer and cigarettes, I realized that feeling like a failure was my messy room, my *big* problem.

In practically all areas of my life, I had been trying to fix things so huge that they felt wholly impossible. Take, for example, my pattern of getting into relationships that weren't good for me only to ultimately have them break down in very dramatic ways that sent me running away to the next performing job that wasn't exactly on my vision board.

One of the early dumbasses who helped in shaping this pattern was when my first live-in boyfriend once got so mad at me for not answering his text messages while I was in rehearsal for an off-Broadway show that he left me a voicemail telling me that his brother had died. When my boyfriend didn't answer my very frantic phone calls a few hours later, I texted various members of his family, including his mother, about how sorry I was to learn about his brother's passing and asking them to help me get a hold of my boyfriend—only to find out that he had lied. No one had died . . . with the exception of him now being dead to me.

I quickly packed my things and made haste, despite the fact that I had been so excited to add an off-Broadway credit to my résumé. The truth was that the gig just didn't pay enough for me to move out on my own, but rather than standing up for myself and fighting to figure out a way to stay in the show, I sheepishly texted the director that he could give my role to my understudy because I had made the decision to leave the city. After that, I found myself doing a children's theatre tour, where I made $200 a week (which wasn't great money even in 2009), drove from town to town in a van with the rest of the cast, and stayed in one-star hotels. It wasn't all bad, though—every now and then a hotel gifted us with a room door that actually locked!

While the gig resulted in less pay and a much less prestigious credit for the ol' rezzy than the off-Broadway gig, it *did* allow me to run away from my problems. This was the first time I allowed a relationship to blow up my confidence (and my career), but it wouldn't be the last.

Eventually this repetitive chain of events led me to singing on cruise ships, where the gig became my version of that gaslighting ex you keep going back to, not because they're good for you, but because the sex (or, in this case, the money) is great. While traveling the world has truly been one of the biggest highlights of my life, leaving the country for eight months at a time meant that I was constantly pushing myself eight months further away from the life I had envisioned.

This merry-go-round-from-hell pattern I created for myself put me in a constant state of turmoil, and it also steered me to drowning my frustrations and embarrassment with alcohol. And, Bestie, I'm not talking about a couple glasses of wine one or two nights a week. Oh no, if day drinking were an Olympic sport, I'd have a gold medal, bitch.

And that's the short version of how I came to find myself in that New Jersey hotel room where the voice of my inner-saboteur flooded my head as I asked *why?* It was telling me that I wasn't good enough, that this was the life I was going to have to accept, and that I did not deserve the things I'd always dreamed of. But in a moment of clarity when that bitch-ass inner-saboteur stopped rambling long enough for me to take a breath, I thought to myself, *What would you say to your bestie right now if she were saying these things about herself?* Because one thing I've always been confident of is that I am a damn good friend.

And I knew exactly what I would say: I would tell her that she deserved the world, that she was capable of doing anything she put her mind to, and that she better throw those stinky-ass sweatpants in a washing machine because nobody likes a smelly queen. So why couldn't I take my own advice?

Everyone, including cliché wall art, likes to say "starting is the hardest part," and as much as I hate cliché wall art, I did it anyway. Instead of trying to fix everything overnight, I decided to start small. Learning to tell myself, "It's okay, bitch," whenever things didn't go my way (instead of destroying a bottle of whiskey in response) was the equivalent of picking up my clothes. And that was exactly my first move: to get sober. It was a starting point to begin loving myself and get my life moving in the right direction. I didn't suddenly have all the answers, and I still had plenty of other ways to numb myself from the pain I felt. But each day I chose to pick up a sock and put it away.

So, Bestie, what's cluttering your messy room? Do you lack confidence? Have you started to feel like you've lost your identity to the ever-growing list of responsibilities and roles you fulfill for others? Are you trying desperately to figure out why a society that asks so much of you—to be a caretaker, nurturer, romantic partner, and more—still has you feeling like you don't matter?

Every time you look around and find your room is a mess, just return to that simple but revelatory question: *Why?* You can think of the answer to each why as an item in your room that needs to be tidied up. Keep asking that same question until you find your way to the root cause of the problem. Here's what it can look like:

I feel like a failure. *Why?*

Because I'm not where I thought I would be in life. *Why?*

Because I haven't gotten the promotion I want at work. *Why?*

Because I haven't applied. *Why?*

Because I don't believe I'll get it. *Why?*

Because I put too much pressure on myself.

Ding-ding-ding! With every answer you receive to each *why*, you're unveiling a layer of yourself, like peeling an onion, only less stinky and with way more self-discovery. Now, rather than feeling overwhelmed with how off track your life might feel, you have an understanding of how you got to where you find yourself today—which means you also understand what has to change to get yourself back on track.

I know it's not exactly fun to admit to yourself that the thing standing in your way is *you*. I was a literal alcoholic to avoid facing that fact. But taking the time to reflect and figure out why I was unhappy led me to the conclusion that *changing my life is my own responsibility*. I would give my best friend the same advice, and the same goes for you. Doubt will creep in. But just because you have doubts about whether you can change doesn't mean you can't.

We all have that big-footed bitch voice in our head that I like to refer to as the inner-saboteur. She'll come out and tell you that you can't, or that you won't, or that you shouldn't. I never thought I would truly be able to give up alcohol because that voice kept telling me I couldn't. I never thought I could let go of these fuck-ass boys who could have been ghosted by their own reflection, but as I write this, I am six years beyond that New Jersey hotel room, I haven't had a drop of alcohol since, and I have found my happily ever after.

I want to tell you that things *can* get better. If you find yourself in a *How the Fuck Did I Get Here?* moment, know that it's an opportunity to figure out why you're here so that you can make a change. It's the chance to pivot and move in the direction you actually want to be going in because, listen, if you already knew what the problem really was, if you knew what was holding you back, you probably wouldn't be here in the first place. Whatever your big problem is in this moment, whatever it is that's holding you back from loving yourself and building the life you want, I can promise you that it's really the summation of a lot of smaller problems. If you can just make your way down to specific pain points, then you can take actionable steps toward solving them.

Doubt is a part of the process, but it's not the end of the journey. Take it from me: You are stronger and more capable than you think. This very moment can be your start. So, I want you to take my hand, unclench your butthole, vow to be your own bestie, and ask yourself *why*?

“Reflecting on how you got here, to this exact moment, can help you get to where you want to go.”

CHAPTER 2

LIKE ELSA SAID: LET IT GO

Hey, Bestie! Let's get one thing straight. You are Barbie, bitch. Classic, collectible, loved by all, and ever evolving. Plus, your legs are to die for in a pair of hot pink stilettos. You are not meant to fade away. No, not *you*. You deserve to slay at every stage of your life.

One of the most important choices you can make in the journey you are embarking on is to let go of the negative feelings other people, and consequently you, have assigned to you. Instead of spending so much time living under the belief that you are damaged, or not good enough, or unworthy, I want you to spend some time figuring out *why* you feel that way.

I learned how powerful taking the time to figure this out can be from my best friend, Kate. I see her as smart, funny, brave, loyal, and kind. She used to describe herself as broken, fat, and worthless. "It is what it is," she would shrug and say after talking shit about herself. I hate that saying because we absolutely have more power over our life than that.

I always wondered where the disconnect between what I saw when I looked at Kate and what she saw when she looked at herself came from. From our countless heart-to-hearts about how she wanted to be a school counselor to help kids grow into their potential, to how she thought she was going to be an amazing wife one day, I knew Kate understood she was a good and deserving person. But something was stopping her from breaking the chains of self-loathing that kept her shackled to the earth instead of soaring to her potential. It wasn't until I met her family several years into our friendship that it all finally made sense.

Growing up, my family spent every Thanksgiving at my nana and papa's house, where my immediate family, aunts, uncles, and cousins all bounced back and forth between the big, long table in the dining room and the living room, where the Macy's Day Parade played on the TV. My memories of these holidays include delicious home-cooked food, playing with the other kids in my family, cozying up to watch *A Christmas Story*, and sneaking off into the back room, where I would take sips of the table wine. To this day, I have a very vivid memory of my nana and mother literally crying with laughter because my little six-year-old gay ass was wine drunk. Apparently, I was a little wino even back then! (After that, the jug of wine was kept in a more secure location.) For me, the holidays were about comfort, family, togetherness, and love.

I figured every family enjoyed a similar holiday dynamic until one Thanksgiving, when I couldn't make it home and Kate invited me to spend the holiday with her family instead. Unlike the usual cozy chaos I was used to, that year it was just me, Kate, her mom, and her stepfather.

Now, I have to say, Kate's mom is fantastic in the kitchen; her food is good enough to make you go "*biiiiiiiiiiiiiiitch*." And we did watch the parade. Though that's about as far as the holiday spirit went. I was stunned to find that the entire day was a barrage of nitpicking and complaints from Kate's parents. Nobody was spared. Broadway performers were called "heifers"; her stepdad commented, "So I guess you stopped that calorie counting business? That's too bad," as Kate scooped mashed potatoes onto her plate; and even I was told to stand up straight because I looked "girly." (Which, I mean, is fair, because I do sit into my right hip, but if Kate's mom thought she could knock 24 years of gay out of me, she was mistaken.)

There wasn't a lot of laughter, meaningful conversation, or any traditions to glue the family together. It felt like being at an office holiday party everyone was obligated to attend. They were doing their due diligence and showing their faces so they could hurry up and leave. I was so fucking relieved to escape the awkwardness when Kate finally said the magic words, "You wanna go back to the city?" Um, *yes*!

As we were leaving, she gave her mom a hug and said goodbye to her stepfather. I thanked them for inviting me and truly meant it when I told Kate's mom she made the best stuffing I had ever tasted. Her mom just kind of scoffed in response, turned to her daughter, and said, "Hopefully next year you'll have a decent job and won't have to come here."

How . . . loving?

If you are one of my social media besties, I'm sure you're salivating, waiting to hear how I destroyed these two people and set them straight. But the truth is, I didn't say anything. This was well before I came into my own power, back when I excused bad behavior in favor of being "nice" and "polite" (trust me when I tell you that I have now come to loathe the idea of "being nice"—but we'll put a pin in that for now). Still, that horribly awkward Thanksgiving *did* give me great insight into why perfectly wonderful humans can go into the world thinking others will judge them harshly based on what they look like, or wear, or how they stand like a girl.

After we left, I thought a lot about what absorbing 24 years' worth of criticism about yourself and the world around you would do to your self-esteem. No wonder people don't believe me when I tell them others aren't sitting there judging you as much as you think. They probably want to say, "Have you met my mother?"

There was a clear shift in our relationship after Kate allowed me a behind-the-scenes peek into her family dynamic. It seemed like she felt a lot more comfortable telling me about moments in her childhood that had stuck with her, manifesting into doubt and self-sabotage over the years—something I could easily relate to. We developed an even deeper friendship as we leaned on each other and learned to stand in our own power. As more time passed by, I watched my best friend explode into an unapologetic and unrelenting version of herself.

The point I'm trying to make is that I always saw a beautiful woman in my friend, and until I met her family, it didn't make sense to me that she couldn't see what I did. But after meeting her mom and stepdad, I realized Kate had been conditioned by her parents' criticism to see and think all of these negative things about herself that had nothing to do with who she actually was. It wasn't an overnight revelation, but eventually Kate realized that she didn't have to hold on to her mom's voice in her head (which is doubly great because her mom smokes, like, a pack of cigarettes a day and her voice sounds like an old lawn mower trying to start up). Slowly, she absorbed the positive things I pointed out about her, all of those sparkly things that made her my best friend.

Here's another thing: It would have been really easy for Kate to get to a point where she blamed her parents for the feelings and struggles she had to contend with in life based on the negative self-talk she inherited from them. But she was determined to take accountability for her own life, and that also included acknowledging the fact that, for a while, she had allowed her parents to change how she felt about herself.

She was no longer a child that lived under her mom's roof and, therefore, her rules. *She* allowed her parents to talk to her the way they did; *she*, for a while at least, gave up trying to define herself as an adult and accepted the criticism her mom doled out, defining herself by that.

After many sessions with her therapist and probably just as many bestie chats with me, Kate told me that she was finally ready to recognize that it wasn't her fault that she was in a less empowered place as a child. She knew that she deserved better. She wasn't that little girl anymore. This put all of the power in Kate's hands because from there, she realized she *also* had the power to change and to set clear boundaries with her parents—which she did.

Today, Kate will immediately end a phone call the moment her mom has a single shitty thing to say. Kate has also worked so hard to unlearn all the negative talk that used to chatter away in her head and instead hypes herself up like she's Beyoncé herself. One of the cutest things I have ever seen is Kate walking up to her mirror and giving herself a high-five before going on a first date. When I asked her if she just high-fived herself she said, "Yeah! I do it all the time because it's my way of telling myself I can do anything." Kate gave herself the gift of letting go of what other people thought about her and decided to figure out for herself what was holding her back so she could do something about it.

I know that cutting ties with people or setting boundaries can feel like negative energy, even if these people treat you like gum stuck to the bottom of their shoe. But watching Kate take back the time she spent feeling deflated by people stomping around in her head like a noisy upstairs neighbor, I saw just how much more time she had for positive relationships with others and, most importantly, with herself. And *that's* all good energy. Maybe for you, the boundaries might have to be more severe, but the beauty of it is that the decision is yours and yours alone to make.

As I write this, Kate just had her second child a few weeks ago. He still looks like a little alien. Kate posted a photo of her son on social media to let her friends and family know that they were both happy and healthy. The first comment I saw on the post was from her mom. It read: "Oh, don't post this picture! The dark circles under your eyes are awful." Charming, right?

Well, I'm not the man I was at 24, and definitely not nearly as concerned about being "nice," so I replied to her comment with, "Ewwwwuhhhh. Or you could just congratulate your daughter for giving birth to your grandchild." This heifer replied to my comment—remember, this is all public under her daughter's photo—with, "Well, she looks like a crack whore."

Well, Bestie, here is the Misha you know! I replied, "Well, in your profile picture it looks like you never learned about sunscreen because you look like a vandalized sweet potato."

So, Bestie, much like my real-life bestie Kate, I want you to identify what you need to let go in your life, and then set that bitch free! Whether it's a person, job, situation, or anything else, free yourself from the weight it adds to your life.

The time has come to break that nasty habit of caring too much about the people and things that hurt or deplete you. I think we are *all* consumed with holding on to ideas of what we think the people in our lives could or should be, rather than seeing and accepting what they truly offer. Like Kate, who was holding on to the idea of what a mother is supposed to be and allowed that idea to open her up to constant emotional turmoil.

I want to be clear. Kate loves her mom and they are very much still in each other's lives. But love does not have to be edgeless. Sometimes you have to sharpen your blade and trim the fat. The boundaries that she has created in her relationship with her mom have given Kate the ability to accept the good and create hard lines around the negative behaviors that hurt her.

Now it's your turn. Here's your action for this week. I want you to grab your journal, open your notes app on your phone, or, hell, whip out some lipstick and a napkin—I don't care what you use, just write this down: *Who or what have I allowed to make me feel bad about myself?* And I want you to really think about it and be honest. It's not about blame here; it's about getting some clarity. And then, once you see it spelled out for you, I want you to ask: *Why did I let this sink in? What good has it caused?* And most importantly, *Do I still want this person or thing to have a seat at my table?*

Now you can take a breath. Think about all the time and energy and confidence you can get back if you stop shrinking yourself because you've filled someone else's mold of you. Envision what it would look like if you reinvested that energy into things that bring you joy, things that nurture you. Your creativity and your peace are what I want you to think about. Now write down what would bring you that too. That's your new vision.

Next, I want you to firmly, yet lovingly, set one boundary based on this vision. Say no to one thing that doesn't fit into your new vision and say yes to one thing that feels like freedom. It doesn't have to be an inconceivable life-altering thing. Just something that makes you feel good about yourself. This is you giving yourself permission to take back your magic.

I'm going to be real with you. Setting boundaries seems like a cute concept on glittery Instagram posts, but the reality is that oftentimes the people you need to be setting boundaries with are the ones sitting at your kitchen table, calling you their best friend, and even sharing your bed. Coloring outside of the lines someone else has drawn for you isn't just walking away from toxic strangers, it often means lovingly stepping back from the expectations put on you by people you deeply care about. These people mean well most likely, but they probably don't really see you. And this can be hard, it can feel like betrayal. But I really want you to hear me when I say this: Honoring who you actually are is not a betrayal. And if someone truly loves you, they'll learn to love the version of you that makes you feel more complete.

I won't lie to you—this takes practice. Telling people they negatively impact you, saying no to things you've said yes to or put up with before, and, hell, even unfriending your eighth-grade bully, can be uncomfortable and will probably feel super awkward. But I promise that feeling will pass. I want you to constantly remind yourself that you can put yourself first and still be a good person. So go be like Elsa and let it go . . . and then go take a nap. You deserve it!

“The time has
come to break
that nasty habit of
caring too much
about the people
or things that hurt
or deplete you.”

CHAPTER 3

STOP PLAYING HIDE-AND-SHRINK

Hey, Bestie! I have a question: Do you turn into the human equivalent of a double-knotted shoelace every time you receive a compliment? Have you ever preemptively apologized, saying something along the lines of, "This is going to be a dumb question, but . . ."? Do you let your inner-saboteur keep you on the sidelines, clutching your blankie in an attempt to protect yourself from embarrassment and failure? If any of this sounds familiar, you're definitely not alone. I've been guilty of holding back and being my own worst critic more times than I can count.

The good news is that this whole self-sabotage thing is a learned behavior—and anything learned can also be unlearned. Part of my own journey toward self-confidence has involved figuring out why my inner dialogue was so negative. In that process, I came to a big realization: While being a walking pile of self-doubt was certainly *part* of what fueled my negative self-talk, that inner-saboteur of mine was also a form of self-defense. If I could judge myself before anyone else got around to doing so, or if I claimed that I couldn't do something before even trying, I could minimize the chances of being hurt by others or failing.

Just to be clear, I didn't realize that these behaviors were a defense mechanism in a single dramatic, thunderbolt moment of epiphany; the lesson just finally sank in after years and years of learning the hard way that beating myself up, being my own worst critic, and staying on the sidelines for fear of failing weren't actually keeping me safe at all. In fact, they usually did the opposite.

While I often had a hard time seeing my own inner-saboteur at work, I can usually see it pretty easily in others. Which brings us to Patrick. I met Patrick one summer many years ago when I was working at a small theatre in the Middle of Nowhere, Pennsylvania. Imagine the movie *Dirty Dancing*—you know, the resort, the drama, the questionable dance moves—and you'll be pretty close to what that theatre experience looked like (minus any dramatic moments that involved wire hangers, of course). Being secluded away from the life and chaos of New York City meant that my castmates and I had to rely on each other and the bond we created.

This particular show had a large cast. We were performing *Happy Days, the Musical*, which was based on the 1970s sitcom of the same name. I played Richie Cunningham, of course, because I'm what? A STAR! But aside from my dazzling performance, what really made this show stand out was how quickly the cast bonded. We all worked so well together onstage, and everyone was more than happy to follow my nightly suggestion that we play beer pong in the cast house after work. Sorry to disappoint you, Bestie—I wasn't yet sober, and I also wasn't always a good influence.

Enter: Patrick. Patrick was a fellow actor, and the only exception to our otherwise close cast. As is true for any social group, there were unwritten rules for how everyone was expected to behave . . . and Patrick broke almost all of them. Right or wrong, the cast perceived that Patrick wanted his performance to be noticed over everyone else's. He was highly critical of the cast members' performances, and more often than not, he refused to socialize with us outside of work.

The final nail was hammered into Patrick's social coffin when one day he very directly stated that he was the most talented person in the cast. This was a huge social no-no. From that moment on, the pleasantries were gone, he wasn't invited to hang out anymore, and he became a big topic of discussion among the rest of the cast. The whole situation was giving, "YOU CAN'T SIT WITH US!" The funny part—to me, at least—was that none of this seemed to bother Patrick. In fact, it was almost like he expected to be the outcast. But, Bestie, if you know anything about me, you know that this whole situation bothered *me*. Even though I sometimes gossiped and got caught up in the drama surrounding Patrick, I still couldn't help but feel bad for him.

One night everyone decided to go out to a local bar because we were off the following day. Although I was usually the instigator of debauchery, I decided to stay home on that particular evening. Could this be the start of sober Misha? Not a chance—that was still years away at this point. But still, I made the choice to hang back because I felt so guilty that Patrick was the only person who wasn't going to join in.

I told the cast that I felt tired and watched as all of the fun people walked out the door toward a night of whiskey shots and making the locals uncomfortable with outbursts of song and dance. As the door shut behind them, I turned to Patrick. "Ten bucks one of them gets beaten up tonight," I said. Patrick chuckled, and I seized that moment as an opportunity to invite him to have a drink and watch a movie with me. I was so used to him turning down any extracurricular social invites that I almost didn't believe it when he muttered, "Sure."

Before Patrick could change his mind, I ran to the kitchen to make us some drinks, then quickly joined him in the living room. We turned on the TV, which really only served as background noise because I immediately started chatting. I wanted to get to know Patrick. The only thing the two of us had in common was the show, so I started talking about that.

The thing is Patrick was going to Patrick, so he immediately started complaining. Rather than giving in to my knee-jerk reaction (which was to recoil at his negativity), I just listened. He talked about how he was dismayed about flaws in his performance so minor that, honestly, no one had even noticed. As I listened, I found myself relating to Patrick because I'm also a perfectionist. I couldn't help but notice that even most of his "notes" about other people's performances usually came back to how they managed to make *him* look bad onstage—or, at least, how he perceived they made him look bad.

The more I listened, the more I began to realize that Patrick wasn't talking shit because he was a dick. He was talking shit because he was insecure. He was pointing out mistakes, no matter how small, before anybody else had the opportunity to, projecting about reasons the audience might not like the show, and then justifying how it wasn't *his* fault. Up until this moment, I had viewed Patrick as egotistical. Suddenly I understood that there was much more at play. So I tried something new.

When Patrick brought up how he had bombed a piece of choreography so devastatingly that it ruined the entire show for the audience—as he saw it, that is—I chimed in. "That reminds me!" I said. "I've been meaning to tell you that the moment when you sing that short solo is one of my favorite things in the show. Your voice is perfect for it!"

I watched as Patrick's face flushed. He seemed to take a moment to consider the compliment. Finally, he replied, "Oh, wow! That means a lot coming from you. I practiced that line over and over again." I could tell he felt really proud of himself.

Now, I know you might be thinking that I could have been feeding a narcissist's ego. But I didn't offer up the compliment because I felt like Patrick was fishing for one. Quite the opposite, I could tell that a compliment was the last thing he expected. And, as it turned out, that single compliment created an opening between us.

After seeing this more vulnerable, human side of Patrick, I made it my mission to integrate him into the group more. Over the next couple of weeks, anytime I heard someone say something snarky about Patrick, I replied that I thought he was just a little misunderstood. When the cast went out, I tried to find a moment away from the group to personally invite Patrick to join us. Honestly, it didn't really work. Patrick's insecurities remained, and any time I vouched for him, he proceeded to make some offhand comment that kept everyone wary of him. He was different with me, but that softer side of him didn't extend beyond our relationship; it was like he couldn't help himself. But whereas I initially thought his comments were rude or mean-spirited, now I understood that they were a shield. Patrick was deflecting others before they could reject him. Unfortunately, he was so focused on protecting himself that he couldn't see the openings that were being offered to him.

I wasn't ready to give up, though. Despite the fact that he continued to be the same ol' Patrick with the rest of the cast, I was struck by how differently he acted with me ever since the night when he realized I was a safe person. I wondered how I could make that same shift happen for everyone else. Then I had a stroke of brilliance! Patrick's birthday was coming up in a few days, so I came up with a simple plan. I printed out a picture for each cast member of a moment in the show that Patrick was in and instructed them to write about a positive memory or a time when Patrick's performance impressed them on the back of the photo. Before the afternoon matinee on Patrick's birthday, I showed up to the theatre early with the stack of photos singing his praises and placed them at his dressing room station along with the cake we had all pitched in for.

"What's this mess?" Patrick muttered when he arrived. Because I was coming to understand Patrick, his reaction made me laugh. He sat down and silently sifted through the photos, flipping each of them over to read the notes his peers had written for him.

Over the next hour, I watched cast members come in and wish Patrick a happy birthday. Because my Virgo ass notices everything,

I smiled as I watched him go from *extremely* uncomfortable to only *mildly* uncomfortable with the positive attention.

So how did this change the course of Patrick's summer? Well, Bestie, real life doesn't always look like a predictable rom-com where we immediately know every plot point and ending. In *that* version, Patrick would have become the most popular person in the cast—the most basic girl ever that everyone still loves for some reason. But the reality is that even after he softened a bit, not everyone took the time or could get to a place where they understood him. Yes, the mob mentality of viewing him as the odd one out definitely subdued, but some people had already made up their minds about him—and that's just the truth of life. But what *did* change is that two other girls in our cast got to see a different side of Patrick on his birthday and, in turn, became open to seeing him in a more favorable light. For the remainder of that summer, the four of us went on to enjoy many nights laughing and making memories around the firepit.

I definitely noticed Patrick's defense mechanisms for what they were, in part, because I'm an empath. But I think I was also drawn to him because I recognized something familiar in him that also exists in me, even if it manifests in different ways: the negative inner voice that says I'm not enough, that makes me believe everyone else is judging me and somehow separates me from everyone else. And the best way to trauma bond with someone is over a common enemy! LOL. I still think about Patrick a lot, especially as I've become aware of the ways in which my own inner-saboteur can make me disrespect myself and, sometimes, even others.

I know I was a good friend to Patrick, but I'm also sure I could've been a better friend to him, just like I've become a better friend to everyone in my life since I've learned to befriend myself. I personally don't believe it's possible to be a good friend to others if you can't be your own friend first. I don't mean that you can't love others and want the best for them, but I think it's only once you begin to take care of yourself the way you want to be loved that you can *truly* understand what love feels like and pay it forward from there. Once you put yourself first, it's like your heart bursts open and overflows to everyone around you.

If you're finding it hard to befriend yourself, think about the people you care about. Consider the ways in which selling yourself short might limit not only your growth and potential, but also your relationships and the love you're able to give. Think about how the world around you will benefit when you choose to love yourself. It's like that airplane analogy: Put your own mask on first. Because what good is a dead bitch? Similarly, imagine how much love you could give to others if you were filled up yourself.

When I think back to Patrick and to previous versions of myself, I realize how much self-doubt can cloud our vision, almost like it's fogging up a mirror. Sometimes it takes hearing from others that we've been more than enough all along. I'm so glad that, on some level, I was able to do that for Patrick . . . and I'm grateful to the people who have been able to do that for me.

So here's a little challenge for you: I want you to think of the compliments you've received over the years, the ones that made you smile, even for a moment. Did you *really* hear them, or do you just remember them? Or did you deflect them like a dodgeball in gym class? If you didn't really hear them, if you didn't allow them to seep in, and if you didn't truly accept them, why don't you try doing that right now? What if you really *believe* it the next time someone tells you that you're smart, funny, kind, and that you have an ass a quarter can bounce off of? What if you choose to override self-doubt and let those words shape how you see yourself, rather than reverting back to what that boring ass inner-saboteur has to say? Just like Patrick and me, you might find that the world already sees your light. You might see that you can lay your self-defenses down because, admit it, they're heavy!

Here's what I want you to do:

1. Make a list of five compliments that have stuck with you over the years, even if you didn't fully believe them at the time.

2. Next to those compliments, write out what your inner-saboteur said in response, or how that shady bitch interpreted the compliment.

3. Here's where you show up for yourself. Write a rebuttal. Yup, cuss out that saboteur. Pretend you are defending your best friend. Be fierce. Be honest. Be kind.

4. Finally, I want you to take one of those compliments and make it your personal affirmation for an entire week. Say it in the mirror, write it in your journal, say it out loud every time you feel yourself slipping into that self-protection mode.

This is how you lay down your armor of sarcasm, perfectionism, or even aloofness that you've used to protect the softest parts of yourself. Just like Patrick, you might realize that your defenses didn't actually protect you, they just kept people out. And, Bestie, the world wants in.

You can hide or shrink yourself because that nasty inner-saboteur likes to convince you that you don't deserve much—or you can go into the world with your full chest. Notice which version of yourself you're choosing to bring into each situation in your life and consider whether that version of you is helping your confidence or hurting it. I know this may not feel like a choice but, trust me, it *is*. Confidence takes practice.

“Consider the ways in which selling yourself short might limit not only your growth and potential, but also your relationships and the love you’re able to give.”

CHAPTER 4

HIGH HEELS, HIGH NOTES, AND HIGHER STANDARDS

For me, childhood was . . . strange. Throughout my little gay life, I had to adapt and blend in, not only to make myself more palatable, but also to minimize risk to my safety. Along the way, I picked up a bad habit of changing who I was anytime I felt uncomfortable.

My dad was in the military when I was growing up. As you may know, the military is rich in macho culture and poor in accepting anything outside of that—and that was especially true in 1993. My dad didn't make very much money in the military, so when I was six years old my mom got a job at a fast-food restaurant to help our family out. This meant that someone had to watch me and my younger sister while my mom was working. Another army wife who lived in the same military housing unit as we did and had two kids of her own around my and my sister's ages offered to help out.

From what I can remember, my sister and I liked the woman who babysat us. When we were there, we got to watch cartoons, play, and run out to the ice cream truck (I can still feel the excitement of that sprint!). One day while we were at this sitter's house, I snuck into her bedroom and went into her closet. I looked around, knowing I shouldn't be in there, and my eyes landed on a pair of nude-colored high heels. They weren't Louboutins, but they *were* a gateway to fabulousness. I pulled them out and put them on. Even though they were comically large on my tiny little feet, I proceeded to stomp down the runway (aka the hallway) to the kids' room, where my friends and sister were playing.

I sat down feeling like a superhero because I was four inches taller and wearing grown-up shoes, and I proceeded to play with a Polly Pocket—probably telling Polly that she was a boss-ass bitch and didn't need a man. LOL. I was having a perfectly lovely afternoon until the babysitter came in and saw me sitting in the middle of the floor in her nude kitten heels (which I wouldn't be caught dead in today, by the way) playing with a "girl's" toy.

I saw the expression in her eyes change from the comforting "mom" eyes I was used to, to what looked like *fear.* "WHAT DO YOU THINK YOU'RE DOING?!" she yelled as she yanked her shoes off my feet like they were the last pair at a Walmart Black Friday sale. I felt confused and ashamed. Here was the same woman who played with me, who took care of me on days when I was sick, and who gave me quarters for that ice cream truck when my parents didn't have any to spare, scolding me for being a "sissy" and telling me that I was a boy, which meant I needed to play with boy toys.

In addition to the confusion, a red-hot wave of shame crashed over me. I *liked* playing with the boy toys . . . but I also liked playing with that boss bitch Polly and whipping up a sweet treat in the Easy-Bake Oven. Why couldn't I do both? The girls didn't get yelled at when they played with the Matchbox cars.

From that day on, I didn't dare go into our babysitter's closet ever again, and I was careful to stick with the toys that didn't have a hint of pink or purple on them. All I ever wanted to do was to make people happy, and if I was going to do that, I would have to figure out a way to change. No matter how careful I was, though, the shame of that moment stuck with me. That day I learned there was something inside of me that I needed to hide from grown-ups. And I was taught something that I wouldn't have the words for until many years later: I thought I had to *earn* love. Because the real me—the fabulous, curious, sparkly me—was wrong, or at the very least, inconvenient. So I didn't just learn to hide. I learned to perform. To please.

In case it's not obvious by now, I'm a firm believer that the more we take accountability for our own lives, the more likely we are to achieve happiness. It's like owning a pair of killer heels: No one can walk in them for you. Part of taking that kind of accountability is unapologetically owning who you are and stomping down the runway of self-love, because the more true to yourself you are, the more fulfilled you will feel. And if you don't think having this amount of love for yourself applies to you, I want you to put your hand over your heart. Right now. Do you feel your heart beating? That's enough to make you feel worthy—beginning with your own love.

The problem with not figuring out and owning who you are (and then loving that version of you) is that you run the risk of becoming something dreadful: a *people pleaser.* There are many ways we can accommodate the world to our own detriment, but one of the most chronic is making like a chameleon and changing who you are based on the environment you find yourself in.

Look, I get it because I spent a lot of my life in a perpetual costume change, adjusting who I was to whatever room I found myself in. It's okay if you find yourself doing this too; I think we all do, so don't go self-flagellating! But what I'm saying is that life has a way of conditioning us to hide the unique pieces of who we are or the parts of us that we feel fear, guilt, or shame about. I want you to recognize when you're doing that, figure out why, and then knock it off. Go back to that heartbeat.

Throughout my childhood, there were countless times when I became a chameleon, assuming a different version of myself to either hide who I was or to make other people feel more comfortable. In addition to the kitten heels, life kept throwing an ever-growing list of things at me that were deemed unacceptable for a young man to wear, do, or be. Being a flamboyant kid in a small town meant that I constantly had to think about how I was standing, or if my voice sounded too girly, or if doing the things that brought me joy would make other people hate me.

Eventually, this habit of morphing into an apologetic version of myself crossed over from childhood into my adult life. After I dropped out of college and moved to New York City, I spent 12 years pursuing a theatre career. I learned rather quickly—both from things casting directors said to me and from having eyes and ears—that talent alone wasn't going to get me where I wanted to go.

I wasn't all biceps and stupidity, I didn't have a manly speaking voice or presence, and I wasn't exactly oozing manly sexuality. And so I watched far less accomplished singers and actors soar to the heights I dreamed of because they were hot and had a deep voice.

Every time I walked into an audition I was consumed with how I was being perceived. I agonized over how I must look as I made my way to the center of the room, fixated on how I shouldn't smile too big because that would be a dead giveaway that I wasn't the leading man because I'd want to smooch the leading man. I put endless amounts of pressure on myself to be flawless because I believed that was the only way I could make up for being gay.

Guess what? It didn't work. Well, okay, that's not exactly true. The flawless part *did* work when I sang and hit every single note with more emotion than a gym bro has felt in his whole life. Casting agents frequently told me that I was one of the best singers they'd ever heard, but also that they "just didn't see a part" for me.

The most frustrating thing of all is that not a single casting director ever really explained what they meant by that. In this void of information, I was left to assume it was because I didn't read as heterosexual. You might be tilting your head like a dog trying to understand the strange noise of me saying that being *gay* in the *theatre* was a hurdle, but it really is for some! I know what the stereotype that "theatre kid" has, and it's based in a lot of fact, but the reality of professional theatre is almost all the stories are heterosexual stories, so if the timbre of your voice is too high or your wrist is limp, it's a lot harder to get cast in those lead roles. Of course there is nuance and exceptions to it all, but nevertheless, this assumption led me to overcompensate more and more with each audition, effectively getting me further and further away from showing up honestly.

Nobody ever said it, but I must have reeked of desperation. I couldn't understand why all the hard work I put into my craft wasn't being reflected in my career. The harder I worked, the more insecure I felt.

When COVID hit and the performing arts were shuttered for nearly two years as a result, life as I had known it ceased to exist. Up until that point, social media wasn't something I had ever taken seriously. Instagram was really nothing more than a photo album of my cruise ship and theatre adventures and a way to let my mom know I was still alive. Then one day as I was sitting on the couch with nothing to do, I downloaded TikTok. I loved that it was video format instead of just pictures, and I started telling stories for no reason other than because it felt like an artistic outlet in a time when there weren't many others.

And what do you know? A few weeks later, my first video went viral. I told a story about standing up for myself and watched in utter amazement as thousands of comments came flooding in. These commenters praised me for facing a bully, told similar stories of their own, and enjoyed a petty little laugh. I thought this video was a fluke, a one-time deal, but shortly after that, I posted another story that reached millions of views. Before long, I was gaining tens of thousands of followers a week just by being myself. No masculine makeover needed.

I experienced a rush of excitement I hadn't felt before. Suddenly, I didn't have to hide, tweak, or man-ify myself to succeed.

I was having so much *fun* making and sharing videos because people were connecting with an unfiltered version of me. I had been so tunnel-visioned in what I thought I needed to be in order to get ahead that I hadn't stopped to consider how much I craved recognition just for being Misha. It was so healing to feel seen and accepted for who I was.

In the end, social media allowed me to find success in a way theatre never had. Not only was I enjoying watching my follower count grow, but I also felt something in my stomach that I hadn't felt in a really long time: *passion*.

Bestie, these are some of the ways life has put pressure on me to be versions of myself that weren't totally authentic. But I wonder who has told you, directly or indirectly, that part of you was *too much, too different, too inconvenient*? Maybe it was your creativity, your voice, or your identity. Take note of those moments.

When you look back at those people or moments in your life, you are putting self-reflection into action. And the purpose is so much more than journaling or having a good cry in the shower (although that's therapeutic too). It's about noticing your patterns, giving them a name, and choosing to step outside of them.

Now I want to offer you an invitation. I invite you to stop auditioning for parts you don't want. Build a path that fits you, instead of breaking yourself to fit an already defined path. I want you to be celebrated, not for a performance or persona, but for the badass you are.

If you're not there yet, that's okay. The first step to anything is recognizing what the problem is and finding a way to get past it. Follow the fun, babe! Pay attention to what makes you come alive and invest in that feeling. We can't control the world around us, and it will continue to try to force its opinions on us, but we can give them a sarcastic smile and lean in to our fun.

Okay, now it's your turn, Bestie. I want you to do a quick self-check. Are you proud of yourself? If you didn't immediately shout, "Hell yeah, Bestie!" then let's chat. I want you to remember that you have survived every day leading up to this very moment, no doubt proving that you are capable of some really hard shit along the way. And now I want you to consider whether or not you have been letting other people take some of that power away from you. If not, then you better work, bitch! If you have, here's what I want you to do:

1. *Write down the times you've survived.* Folding to the wants of the world and people around you doesn't make you a weak person. You did what you had to do to get through the day, Bestie. When have those bullies won?

2. *Call them out.* Look back at what you've written and identify who or what the problem was. Who was the bitch with halitosis that made you believe that their idea of you was of greater value than who you really were?

3. *Reclaim your damn power.* I want you to write out why they don't get to hold the power anymore. For example, I would write, "Babysitter, you don't get to dim my light anymore just because you have a narrow-minded worldview. It was perfectly normal for me to be interested in the things that you were, because I felt safe with you. But you robbed me of that feeling."

4. *Set it with a promise.* Make the commitment to yourself that you'll let that shit go and move forward focusing on yourself and if who you are makes you feel good.

You don't have to have all the answers today. You reading this right now means you're ready to start. So I want you to know two things. First: *I'm so damn proud of you.* I see you. I recognize you living through your toughest days, the mundane ones, and everything in between. Second: *It's never too late to change your own narrative.* You don't have to let the past hold your future hostage.

Starting today, I want you to put on your metaphorical (or literal) heels and strut, because the world is your runway and your time is now. Celebrate what you've achieved, dream unapologetically big, and don't ever let anyone convince you that you deserve less. You were made for greatness—now go serve it.

“Build a path that fits you, instead of breaking yourself to fit an already defined path.”

CHAPTER 5

DATE YOURSELF, MAKE IT WEIRD

Hey, Bestie! I consider myself somewhat of a relationship expert because I am the go-to guy when my gal pals finally can't ignore all those red flags Chad has been waving, as if the cargo shorts he wears weren't bad enough (why does he need so many pockets?!). For as long as I can remember, my friends have always come to me for advice, as a sounding board, and as a safe space to vent. I've spent countless hours listening to my friends talk about their dating lives and relationships, so I know how common it is to experience pain caused by the person who is supposed to love you. What's so ironic is that, for a long time, even as I was calling out all of the Chads and Brads, reminding my friends that they could have more and deserved better, I was experiencing the same things they were in my own relationships. Over and over again.

I'll spare you each and every clunker I met along the way, but let's just say that I used to be a chronic serial monogamist who made a habit of ignoring the warning signs of these boys the same way I ignore those extra five pounds I put on every time I go to the Cheesecake Factory. Let's just say I've eaten a lot of cheesecake. But that's in the past and no longer any of my business. Unlike the cheesecake, that merry-go-round of dick (heads) I was on never seemed to result in a newfound respect for myself or the wherewithal to change the pattern I was very clearly stuck in.

Until Evgeni, that is.

Evgeni and I met in rehearsals for one of my cruise ship contracts. He was a Ukrainian ballet dancer. Bestie, really quickly, go google "male Ukrainian ballet dancer" and you'll understand why I was immediately smitten. The only problem was that Evgeni didn't speak English and my Russian was limited to "vodka." We had all the makings of a true love story for the ages!

Over the next few weeks, the two of us flirted as much as our language barrier and Google Translate would allow. Sometimes I got a message from him that said something like, "You're a sexy robot." I'm pretty sure that's not what he was trying to say, but we understood each other well enough and started dating.

The next few months were a whirlwind of Evgeni and I learning each other's languages, traveling to exotic lands on the ship, and me falling absolutely head over heels for him. There was just one tiny problem: Nobody could know about our relationship. He made it very clear that being gay was not "normal" where he was from and that our romance needed to be top secret. Sure, the ballet dancer and musical theatre performer who are always together *definitely* aren't sleeping together. Did I love this arrangement? No. Did I accept it? Sadly, yes.

When our contract finished, we were, unfortunately, unable to do another one together, so Evgeni and I each went off to our next gigs on separate ships. Despite this, we were still together. The two of us spent the next eight months messaging each other every day, promising each other that this separation was only temporary. It seemed clear to me that we were in love, anticipating and excited about our future together. Or so I thought.

When my contract without him neared its final docking, I made the decision to book a ticket on Evgeni's ship to visit him. We would spend eight days together, sailing from Venice to Barcelona. Bestie, this romantic escapade cost me thousands of dollars. But what's a few grand in the name of love and mild delusion?

Finally, the day arrived. I giddily boarded my flight and headed to the gorgeous hotel overlooking one of Venice's iconic canals that I had booked because I'm a romantic bitch.

I paced like a feral cat outside the hotel until, finally, I saw Evgeni walking toward me. At last, we were reunited! It was amazing . . . and also slightly awkward. Like, do we hug? Do we kiss? Or do I just stand here and weep? I felt like my heart was going to fall out of my butt as we walked up the stairs to our room.

And that, my friend, is where the fairy tale ends (insert record scratch here).

The door to the room hadn't even clicked shut before Evgeni asked, "Can you please to looking up fly from Barcelona to Kiev?" I was confused, not because of his broken English, but because I didn't know why he would need a plane ticket in the near future. That's when I learned that he had invited his mother and sister (who speak not a single word of English, by the way) on the cruise. Like, *this* cruise—the same one I'd paid thousands of dollars for so that we could have a reunion so romantic that even Meg Ryan would be jealous.

I could not think of a reason why Evgeni would invite his very homophobic mother to join us on this trip after the two of us had spent so many months apart, but Evgeni explained that he didn't want any of his co-workers to guess that I was his boyfriend because we were staying in my room together. He figured that if he played the role of the perfect heterosexual Ukrainian son by offering up his cabin for his mom to stay in, he had the perfect excuse to stay in my room without anyone getting suspicious. Evgeni: Master of Alibis.

Over the course of the next eight days, I was tortured by being introduced as Evgeni's *friend* over and over again. The first time it happened was immediately after I boarded the ship, when a very pretty girl wearing one of those curly ponytail hairpieces, a full face of makeup (including fake eyelashes that practically tickled me when she blinked), and a tracksuit with the ship's logo on it, came rushing up to Evgeni. She was obviously a dancer in his cast.

"TODAY IS THE DAY! ARE YOU SO HAPPY?! YOUR MOM IS HERE!" she squealed. Then she turned and looked at me. "Oh, hi!" she said. "Who are you?" The look on her face was so neutral that it plunged a knife into my already bruised heart. I smiled politely and promptly excused myself to the nearest bar, where I purchased the all-you-can-drink package.

This bombardment of humiliation and awkwardness continued every time I met a new crew member. When I wasn't hearing the f-word, I was either walking around ports with Evgeni and his mom, doing my best to make small talk in Russian (because that was our only common language), or stuffing my face at the buffet while double-fisting vodka sodas. Drinking by myself at the many bars around the ship and achieving near-comatose levels of inebriation was the only way I could think to find shelter from the insecurity I felt.

But nothing prepared me for the moment when I met a striking gay British dancer in the gym. He and Evgeni were already there when I arrived . . . spotting each other on the bench press. The dancer was mysteriously cold to me and had a distinct I-know-your-boyfriend-better-than-you-do air about him. It was very clear to me that these two were more than just workout buddies. I mean, as the OG secret boyfriend, I knew the signs.

If that happened today, I'd probably deadlift my dignity and hurl a verbal kettlebell straight at their egos. But back then, Bestie, I didn't even confront Evgeni. I was so overwhelmed by my feelings of betrayal and anger that I kept my head down just enough to get through the vacation. But even then, deep down I already knew our relationship wasn't going to have a happy ending. (Cue Meg Ryan in tears.)

Have you ever faced the internal struggle of knowing that things will eventually fall apart, so you make the puzzling choice to just coast along in that broken relationship until it happens? I think it's that our fear of being alone outweighs our sadness in the moment, but seriously, why the hell would our brains do that to us? It's like we can see the iceberg, we know the ship is going down, but instead of getting on a lifeboat, we order another cocktail and hope it'll magically work out. Spoiler . . . it doesn't.

I don't know about you, but I think I was clinging to the fantasy. To the dream of what it could be if everything, and by everything I mean a cheating-ass man, would just fix itself. So if you've ever fooled yourself that you were being strong by staying, when really you were being scared by staying, I just want you to know that you aren't alone.

I was scared of starting over. I was scared of silence. But I promise that staying in a relationship where you are unseen or unchosen is a lot lonelier than being alone.

Yet from the bedazzled shards of my broken heart rose an epiphany—and on Christmas morning at that. It occurred to me that instead of investing all this effort and emotion into relationships, I needed to date myself instead. I set the goal that I would not drink for the next year, and I would also set aside any amount of time I could find on a daily basis that was for me and me alone so that I could get a sense of who I was and what I deserved. I needed a minute to breathe.

That first year of sobriety I poured so much love into myself that I felt more cared for than I *ever* had in any relationship. And I didn't just pamper myself; I also took that time to sit down and do the hard work.

For the first time in my life I reflected on the traumas and pain points I had experienced in the past and tried to understand not only how they had affected me, but also the role I had played in them. *Why did that hurt so much? What was I looking for in these men, and why did I keep choosing guys who didn't give love in return?* I wanted to truly understand what I was looking for before I went back out and started searching for it again.

Bestie, that year was so transformative for me. I didn't realize how discontent I had been. When I was ready to open myself back up to men—I mean, this ass can hold up an entire economy, so who am I to deny its glory to the world?—for the first time, I went on dates without using alcohol as a crutch. There were no longer any boozy safety nets or tipsy flirting, but all the work I'd put into my sobriety and learning who I was made the dates way less scary.

Staying sober on dates also made me more present and clear-minded about the person I was sitting across the table from, which allowed me to make better choices. I met guys who drank too much on a first date, guys who didn't know where they were headed in life, and guys who were perfectly fine but just fizzled out. In the past, I probably would have forced a "spark" between me and any one of these guys, only to end up in an unhappy, unhealthy two-year situationship. But I didn't do that this time. I knew what I wanted and what I didn't want. *New* Me had standards. And New Me kept choosing myself.

I want you to take a second to ask yourself: Are you dating to build a life, something beautiful? Or are you dating to distract yourself from your own reflection? Be honest with yourself, Bestie. There's no shame in admitting that you've chosen people who haven't reciprocated that. It's a universal experience. I've been right there, in that heartbreak with you. The second you quit twisting yourself up into knots to be picked and start standing in your unfiltered truth, that's when real love can walk through the door.

If you have found yourself in that same negative pattern again, I want you to consider taking a break from dating. Not a redownload-the-apps-next-week kind of break either. No, an intentional, soul-deep pause where you can ask yourself who you are when nobody is picking you but you. Give yourself the gift of being the damn priority for once!

I continued to simultaneously date myself and other men for another year and a half until one day I agreed to go on a date with a guy who turned out to be incredibly smart, sober like me, and who lit up when he talked about where he saw himself in the future. He treated me with the utmost respect and care. Could this be? Sparks *and* emotional availability?

Lucky for him that I did all that work on being content with myself so I could patiently wait for him to come into my life. We never stopped hanging out, and now he is my husband. *Awwwwwwwwww.* And you know what else? I still find a moment in every single day that is just for me. A piece of my day that has nothing to do with me as a partner, a son, a co-worker, a friend, or a dog dad—just me. Give me a nice candle and a sparkly bath bomb and I'm in heavenly bliss.

My contentment with who I am has left my cup overflowing, which has freed me to share the excess with my husband. Because I have a healthy balance of loving myself and loving him, I am able to care for him in more healthy and meaningful ways than I knew how to do in past relationships.

So, over to you, Bestie! Whether you are single as a pringle, in a perfectly happy relationship, or wondering what you're doing as you stare into what feels like the black hole that is your future if you stay in your current relationship, I want you to date yourself. I want you to prioritize and care for yourself with the same vigor and energy you care for others in your life.

Here is an easy guide for you to come back and refer to anytime you need. We'll call it your Self-Love Plan. First let's talk about your commitment.

Duration Options:

1. 6-Week Trial Run—If you want to dip your toes into the self-prioritization pond. No pressure, just possibilities, babyyyy!

2. 6-Month Foundation—I think this is juicy. This is a good chunk of time to notice some real changes.
3. 1-Year Glow Up—For the bestie truly ready to fall in love with themselves.

Now here are the steps:

Step 1—Daily You Time. This is non-negotiable. This is that specific moment of your day that is just for you. No people, no distractions, just self-adoration. Some of my favorite options are:

- Sit in your car for an extra 10 minutes and belt out your favorite tunes that make you feel unstoppable.
- Go for a walk without listening to music or a podcast, where it's just you and your thoughts. I *love* doing this!
- You know you bought that skincare serum that's just been sitting on your bathroom counter. Take a few minutes to plump up your "bathroom time" to make you feel like you're taking care of yourself.

The Goal: Build a ritual that teaches your nervous system that you matter. Because you do.

Step 2—Monthly Big Date. Once a month I want you to do something that is a bigger gesture. After all, you are trying to woo yourself. Some of my favorite ways to do this are:

- A good ol' fashioned therapy session. I feel so much less weighed down when I purge everything that has been on my mind. I don't go to therapy for someone else to "fix" me but because I feel better just talking about everything out loud.
- Go to a movie by yourself. Psst! I won't tattle if you sneak some of your own snacks in.

- Buy that thing you've had your eye on for a while. This is my favorite thing to do. I spoil myself rotten. If you have the means, take advantage by recognizing the things you *truly* want and get them.

The goal here is to let yourself know that you are worth effort and investment. You'd want a partner to believe this, so you need to believe it as well.

Step 3—Check-In. No matter what time frame you've chosen to spend on yourself, check in with how you're doing.

- Are you still settling for something anywhere in your life?
- Are you making choices based on fullness or fear?
- What is something you've learned about yourself?

Journal about it or talk to a friend about it. Just don't skip this part.

I want you to hype yourself up while you do this. Dress up in ways that make *you* feel amazing, not what you think others will respond positively to. Look in the mirror and tell yourself the things you love about yourself—sing it loud! It might feel weird at first, but trust me, the weirder the better. Take yourself out on dates, be proud of your accomplishments both big and small, give yourself grace when you make a mistake. Be the perfect partner to yourself. Love yourself, respect yourself, and spoil yourself rotten. Then notice how, over time, this new focus on you starts to create a foundation for the life you want.

When you have a strong foundation within yourself, you won't fall down nearly as hard and will have a much easier time getting up again when life throws you a curveball. Because now, even in those tough moments, you can give yourself the care, comfort, and support you need to get through it and keep on moving along.

And yes, we humans are social creatures, and *of course* we want nurturing relationships with other people—I'm not suggesting you start knitting your next partner out of yarn. But what I *am* saying is that when you give yourself your all, when you take care of yourself and know you can rely on you, then you will raise the bar and choose the people in your life much more thoughtfully. Why would you need to get permission from someone else when you can already give it to yourself?

Choose people to be in your life because they're the *right* people, because they make you happy—not because you're trying to fix something. This is a game changer.

So put on your best outfit and hit the town. Or put on your jammies and curl up on your comfy couch with a good book. Because falling in love with yourself is the biggest plot twist of all. Who knows? Maybe you'll get lucky tonight.

“The second you quit twisting yourself up into knots to be picked and start standing in your unfiltered truth, that’s when real love can walk through the door.”

—Part II—

AFFIRM THE SHIT OUT OF YOURSELF

P*hew!* You did the hard part. You looked in the mirror, faced some messy truths, and admitted where you might have lost parts of yourself along the way. You checked the box on self-reflection. Cute! Now it's time to rebuild. Get ready, because you are about to affirm the shit out of yourself. You are going to step into your power, own your worth, and refuse to let anyone—even your own inner-saboteur—tell you you're anything less than amazing.

This part of the book is all about flipping the script. Maybe confidence doesn't come naturally to you, and that's okay. You can start small. We'll talk about how confidence starts with you choosing yourself, even if that means walking away from people who once felt like home. We'll dive into how confidence means embracing your quirks, your loud laugh, and even your bad decisions. Hey, at least they make for a good story! Confidence isn't reserved for a select few, it is something you can choose to embody.

And sure, affirmations are words you can speak as you look yourself in the eye in the mirror. But they can be much more than that. They are the things you strive to believe about yourself and that you can prove to yourself through action.

So consider this me giving you permission (even though you don't need *anyone's* permission) to slip into your own awesomeness. No more shrinking to make others comfortable. It's time to build yourself back up, piece by piece, until you are standing tall, flipping your hair, and fully embracing the badass you were always meant to be.

CHAPTER 6

FLIP YOUR HAIR, FLIP YOUR MINDSET

Hey, Bestie! I want you to show up like you know you're worthy, even on days you might not fully believe it. But if you don't believe that yet, don't worry. I've learned that sometimes it just takes one moment, one spark, one hair flip to see yourself the way the world should see you, the way I see you—bold, brilliant, and worthy as hell.

Confidence doesn't wait for permission. But if affirming yourself feels like a stretch, stay with me.

I'm sure you've heard the phrase "fake it 'til you make it." Well, I'm proof that it works. Onstage, I had all the confidence in the world—to the point where I almost felt like I was invincible. But offstage was a different story; I felt shy and insecure, reserved and wary. I wanted to feel as I did onstage in other parts of my life as well. And I knew that was possible because even though I was inhabiting fictional characters onstage, it wasn't all an act—there were real parts of me in each character I played. The power I felt when I was singing songs and basking in applause lived inside of me. I wanted to harness that sense of confidence, bravery, and pride in all areas of my life, but unfortunately I couldn't just flip a switch and make it so. At first, I had to fake it until I made it.

I've never witnessed someone take one moment of confidence and run with it quite like my friend Lisa. I met Lisa through a project we were assigned to do together in a college poetry class. Normally group projects made my soul shiver because I had an extreme aversion to frat bros who weren't into finishing their part of a project. Thankfully, Lisa didn't make a habit of doing keg stands on Tuesday nights and took our project as seriously as I did. But as it turned out, we had a very similar sense of humor (10/10 sarcasm) and also, she was *smart*. Like the intimidating kind of smart that makes you want to google big words before responding to texts. In the few days we spent working together, we became fast friends.

One night when Lisa and I were working, we discovered that we were both obsessed with the show *Gossip Girl*. Okay, okay—I admit it: It wasn't the show we were obsessed with, Bestie; it was Penn Badgley. After we turned in our paper (which we got an A on, by the way), we made it a weekly tradition to have a bottle of wine while watching our shared imaginary husband get into whatever weekly drama the show's writers had concocted for him.

As easy as it was to love Lisa, I quickly realized that she didn't have many friends. Although I got to see a fun, charismatic version of her, in most situations she was shy and deeply insecure because she had *alopecia areata*, a condition that made her immune system attack her body's hair follicles, which caused balding. Yes, I've made jokes about terrible men whose hairline starts at the free throw line (because they deserved it), but the truth is that hair loss can be emotionally treacherous and difficult to accept—*especially* for a 19-year-old college girl.

Lisa's alopecia left her feeling self-conscious, isolated, and weighed down, and I think she enjoyed the fact that she didn't feel like "the bald girl" with me. She was just Lisa—hilarious, brilliant, and fun.

I was genuinely curious about her being bald when we first met, and I asked her about it. I didn't avoid looking at it, and I didn't turn it into a joke. I wanted to know her. Isn't that what friendship is all about? Having fun but, also, feeling safe—almost like you've come home.

A few months after Lisa and I met, the theatre department was gearing up to do what it did best: throw a themed party. Think of a fraternity or sorority party, but with stellar production value and consensual sex. As a biology major, Lisa didn't have the same built-in social life that us theatre kids did, and I told her that she *had* to come. She hesitantly agreed, but I think only because she could sense that I wasn't going to take no for an answer.

The week before the big event, we were in a costume shop to outfit ourselves for the party's Dungeons and Drag Queens theme. I could see how unsure she felt as she half-heartedly flicked through items for her own costume. When I pointed out a purple sequin jumpsuit that caught my eye, Lisa shook her head. "That's really loud," she said. "I would feel like everyone's looking at me." I put the garment back on the rack and continued searching.

It was clear that Lisa was getting overwhelmed by the idea of a costume that would make her stand out even more than she already felt she did, so I tried to break the tension by abandoning the sequins and asking her to help me look for a long, straight wig that channeled Cher. Eventually Lisa picked up a Dolly Parton-esque, the-higher-the-hair-the-closer-to-Jesus-style blonde wig. She leaned over, put the wig on, flipped her head up, and spun toward the mirror. Her eyes lit up as the perfectly curled locks fell into place just so.

Wasting no time, I put on my gay best friend hat and shouted, "YYYYYAAAAAAAAAAAASSSSSSSSSS, GIIIIIIIIRRRRRRLLLLLLL!"

Lisa turned this way and that, flipping the ends of the wig and gazing at her reflection. I could tell she felt beautiful, so I pleaded with her to buy the wig for the party.

She stared at herself for a few more seconds, then turned to me. "I'm feeling purple sequins with this." She grinned.

Bestie, I was so happy that my heart burst.

A few nights later, it was time for the party. Throughout the night, Lisa stuck with me and three of my closest friends, including one friend named Kim. Whether it was because of the wig, the realization that the theatre kids aren't scary, or, most likely, because of the accumulation of liquid courage, as the hours went by, Lisa began to loosen up. We flitted between the rooms of the house, danced in the living room, and generally had a blast.

The next week I met Kim at the dining hall between classes. As soon as we arrived, we spotted Lisa standing in line. We went over to say hi, and that was the first time Kim realized that Lisa was "the bald girl" from around campus.

As we sat there munching on our prison-cafeteria-style pizza, Kim asked Lisa if she wanted to join us and a few other friends for a movie night. Immediately, Lisa clammed up. Haltingly, Lisa told Kim what she had told me many times—that she didn't have the confidence to make friends easily and always felt like people were staring at her bare head.

Kim just nonchalantly replied, "Well, you seemed pretty confident when you were dancing at the party in your wig the other night. Why don't you just wear that?"

Lisa didn't end up coming to movie night, but as the two of us were fawning over our favorite gossip girl a few days later, she casually mentioned that she had been researching wigs—the non-Dolly, everyday kind. I asked if I could see some of her choices, and the two of us proceeded to pore over pictures of wigs for hours, envisioning the styles she would look best in. We finally landed on a shoulder-length, swooped bang wig in a warm blonde tone that we thought would make Lisa's eyes pop, be easy to manage, and—most importantly!—make her feel like a pop diva princess. Lisa ordered it on the spot.

Several days later, Lisa texted me to come over immediately. I knew this was serious business because it cost money to text back then (yes, seriously). When I arrived, Lisa greeted me with her new wig on, and I told her what I really thought: She looked beautiful.

Bestie, I have to tell you: I don't know if a fairly cheap, shake-and-go wig has ever impacted *anyone* as much as it did Lisa. She wore that dang wig *out*! From that point on, she walked around campus with her no-longer-bald head held up just a little bit higher, joined my friends and me for a few movie nights, and even made some new friends in her biology classes.

Okay, okay, I know you might be thinking that Lisa shouldn't have needed a wig to feel confident and worthy. But you know what it did do at the time? It allowed her to fake it until she made it.

Have you ever needed a little something? Just one small change to help you step into the version of you that you were becoming? I think of it as borrowing some confidence from the future you until it truly fits. Sometimes it's a wig, maybe a power outfit, or some sassy affirmation you whisper under your breath. The point is, you don't have to have it all together in order to walk into a room as if you do. You just need to show up like you know you're worthy, even on days you might not fully believe it.

I think the "fake it 'til you make it" concept gets misunderstood because people think that it means you're being fake. But I think it means you're building a bridge, or it's like dress rehearsal for the life you deserve until it feels like home. And then magically, one day you're laughing too hard to notice that you aren't faking it anymore. You've made it. You've become her. So throw on the wig, the red lipstick, and walk into the room tits first to do whatever you need to do to get closer to feeling like you.

And you know what, Bestie? It took a few months, but eventually Lisa decided to keep her head as bald as she had been the day I met her. She told me that, yes, it sometimes still felt uncomfortable, but she kept reminding herself that she was the dancing queen at every party she attended and that she made friends easily. *She* was doing all of that, not her wig. She borrowed some confidence from that wig until she got to the place we wanted her to get to in the first place!

So, Bestie, what's *your* wig? Let's break it down into an exercise.

1. Today—Identify your wig. I want you to think of three specific moments when you feel like the absolute baddest, most confident version of yourself. When are you just unstoppable? Are you leading a meeting at work? Making your friends laugh? Baking a homemade pie that would make me drop my panties? These are your power moments.

2. This Week—Analyze the energy. For each of your power moments I want you to write down why you think those versions of you shine so brightly. What are you telling yourself in those moments? Is it what you're wearing, what you're doing, who you're surrounded by? Get as specific as possible. Just like the recipe for that tasty pie you made, the goal is to identify the ingredients of your confidence confetti cake.

3. Over the Next 6 Months—Repurpose the energy. I want you to pick just one area of your life that doesn't come as easily. Public speaking, setting boundaries, asking for help are some examples. And I want you to start "wearing your wig," or borrowing energy from

your power moments. Imagine yourself as you are in those moments and plop that version of you into these less comfy zones. Start small, maybe once a week, and build it from there!

4. All the Time!—Reflect and adjust. By now you know I love a good reflection moment. Routinely check in with yourself and whether you felt more confident in those uncomfortable areas. What helped? What didn't? Adjust the bad bitch! Sometimes we need a messy bun and other times we need a glued-down lace front. It's all about trial and error!

It takes some practice, but the more you focus on allowing yourself to feel confident for whatever reason, no matter how small, the more you draw attention to the things you already love about yourself and the more positivity you will absorb into your being. Do it for long enough, and eventually this sense of confidence will become who you are.

I'm not going to lie: This might feel a bit awkward at first. Imposter syndrome is a bitch. But, as they say—and, yes, I'm cringing as I write this—*dress for success*. Even if it's eye-rolly, it's still true. Wear your best self and keep reminding yourself that you really *are* that person. On the days when it feels hard, I want you to look in the mirror, flip your hair as dramatically as you possibly can, and imagine my little gay ass yelling, "YYYYAAAAAAAASSSSSS, GGGGGIIIIIIIIRRRRRRL!" Because trust me, I am always rooting for you.

Throw on the wig,
the red lipstick, and
walk into the room
tits first to do
whatever you need
to do to get closer to
feeling like you.

CHAPTER 7

YOUR FRIENDSHIP CHECK BOUNCED

The more you feel confident in your own skin, the more you may find that the relationships in your life feel . . . different than they did before. You might even start side-eyeing the people in your orbit who seem to be changing. In reality, though, it's *you* who's changing and who can make relationships that used to work start to feel uncomfortable. And this is not always a bad thing.

That lesson practically bitch-slapped me across the face and called me a slur. It was harsh and eye-opening, and, Bestie, I hope you can avoid a similar situation by remembering that you can still be a good person while also telling someone who is disrespecting you to fuck off.

Let's travel together back to 2018, when I was getting ready to ring in the new year at my friend Courtney's house. I was super uncomfortable on this particular occasion because I was only a week into my sober journey, and New Year's Eve was traditionally *our* holiday. Before that, if there were drinks to be had, bad decisions to be made, or a party to cause a scene at, Courtney and I were there!

Despite the fact that Courtney knew this year's celebrations would be very different from our usual debauchery, she made a huge effort to support me, even if I still felt like a red Solo cup among a sea of champagne glasses. We dressed up in our sparkliest outfits, she made mocktails for me (which I clung to like an emotional support drink), and her dog, Fumo, cuddled me on the couch. And then right before midnight, my phone rang. I looked down to see that Gabby, my best friend from childhood, was calling.

Despite the fact that Gabby was a couple years older than me, the two of us were inseparable growing up in our blink-and-you-miss-it town in upstate New York. We were in school and community theatre together, spent an incomprehensible amount of time hanging out at each other's houses, and got into constant trouble. She was quite literally the *only* person I felt comfortable being myself with. We were the same brand of weird, obsessed with the same things, and—most importantly—she was the *only* person who knew I was gay, even including my very loving parents.

I'm not sure if you've ever kept a secret from 99 percent of the people around you, but if you haven't, I can tell you that having even one person who knows the truth to lean on is enough to drastically change your entire life experience. Gabby allowed me to feel loved and understood, and most importantly, she allowed me to feel *safe*.

Then life happened, as she does. The two of us stayed connected in the way modern adults with busy lives do: through social media, sporadic phone calls, and lots of we-need-to-catch-up! texts, but eventually 12 years passed without seeing each other. But now, here she was calling me and my sequined self while I was soberly sandwiched between a drooling dog and a virgin mojito.

Gabby chirped, "Hi, babe! So, I haven't heard from you and my birthday is coming up. I thought we could get everything planned out."

I had absolutely no idea what she was talking about until she explained that I apparently had called drunk out of my mind a few weeks earlier, telling her we should meet somewhere for her birthday in January. Even though I didn't remember it, I was excited about the idea because what better time to see this safe person in my life than this particular moment, when I could use all the love and support I could get?

Gabby suggested we meet in New Orleans, where she had lived for a brief period a few years ago. Logistically, it made sense, but my newly sober self was wary about the party scene in NOLA. I told Gabby I was okay with the plan but warned her that I had recently given up alcohol so I wouldn't be partaking.

"We'll see," she replied.

Those two words floored me. Bestie, I love you, and if you drink responsibly and don't have a problem with it, good for you! But if someone you know tells you they aren't going to drink anymore . . . don't say that. It's not supportive, and it's not cute.

It was such a foreign feeling to be disappointed in Gabby, and there was a moment when I thought that this trip might not be the best idea, but I really wanted to see my best friend. Also, I was a *baby* (albeit, a super-cute baby) in both my recovery and in choosing to put myself first. At that point, I didn't know how to stand up for myself and tell Gabby we could reconnect once I was in a more stable and safe mindset to do so.

As we planned the trip over the next couple of weeks, Gabby explained that she didn't have a ton of disposable income. We've all been there, girl—broke but full of plans. First, she asked if I could book our Airbnb, promising to pay me her share once we got to New Orleans. A few days after that, she told me some unexpected bills had popped up; she wondered if I'd be willing to buy her plane ticket to New Orleans and promised to pay me back at the beginning of the trip.

Listen, I am not a particularly frugal person (seriously, you should see my shoe closet!) and I would give anything for my friends, so I didn't think twice about doing this for Gabby. After all, I had the money and I loved her.

When I arrived at the Airbnb, I got there early so I could greet her with decorations, a cake, and the presents I had bought for her. Then I waited for Gabby to arrive like an enthusiastic and impatient puppy perched upon a kitchen stool, surrounded by streamers, my fingers sore and callused from tying so many balloons.

When Gabby opened the door, dropped her bags, and ran to me, we greeted each other with the biggest hug I've ever received in my whole life. I swear we didn't let go for, like, five whole minutes. I just knew this was going to be a great week.

After we'd spent some time catching up, I asked Gabby what she wanted to do for her birthday. In response, she walked over to her suitcase and pulled out a bottle of whiskey. She proceeded to fumble through the kitchen, opening every cupboard door until she found shot glasses.

Did you catch that, Bestie? *Glasses.* Plural. She poured two shots and pushed one toward me, beaming like she had just solved world hunger.

I pushed the shot glass away, gently reminding her that I had given up alcohol because my drinking had gotten out of control.

"You were serious?" she asked, incredulously. "You really aren't going to drink for my birthday?"

And there it was: one friend's boundaries slamming into the other one's expectations. I excused myself, saying that I needed to use the bathroom. Instead, I went to my bedroom, where I took a few minutes to remind myself about all the people in my life who were deeply supportive of my decision. I felt a tingle of anger in my chest, but I hated feeling anger back then, so I swiftly shook it off and convinced myself that it was *fine*. Everything was *fine*.

When I emerged from my room, Gabby immediately informed me that she had texted her ex-girlfriend, who would be meeting us at a bar on Bourbon Street in an hour. There had been no mention of an ex-girlfriend in the weeks leading up to this trip, but, once again, I pressed that prickling sensation of anger down and reminded myself that this was Gabby's birthday. I just had to get through one night.

Off we went to a newly sober person's version of Hell, where not only did I have to be around booze, but I was also forced to listen to tone-deaf strangers butcher '90s classics. Not once did my best friend check in on me. Instead, the night consisted of Gabby slamming back shots and various mixed drinks as she reunited with not just her ex, but also seemingly everyone who lived in New Orleans.

After leaving the karaoke nightmare, we bounced around from bar to bar in what felt like an endless loop, until *finally* Gabby and her ex-girlfriend got into a huge fight at 4 A.M. I watched on as they screamed at each other, as did literally everyone else in the bar.

When I woke up the next morning, I figured we would do what best friends do—grab some lunch, catch up, and maybe go shopping. But we didn't do any of those things because Gabby *and* her ex didn't emerge until 4-freaking-P.M. that afternoon. The good news was that they seemed to have made up. The bad news was that the first words out of Gabby's mouth were, "Ugh, I'm so hungover. I need a drink. Let's go to the bar so we can get a strong drink and some food."

As I looked at Gabby, I thought to myself, *I really don't like her.* And yet, I couldn't seem to bring myself to say no to tagging along with her to the absolute last place on earth I wanted to be. I felt conflicted and confused because the truth of the matter is that Gabby was being the girl I had always known: free-spirited, the life of the party, always chasing a good time. The issue was that *I* was no longer the same person.

Every day of the rest of the trip was a repeat of the one before, like a broken record of chaos. And by our final night in New Orleans, I had reached my limit. As Gabby and her ex were mid-fight, I walked up to Gabby—the same person who I had belted out showtunes with, whose shoulder I'd cried on when I finally had the courage to accept the fact that I was gay, and who felt more like a sister than my actual sister did—and said, "I'm going back to the apartment because I have an early flight in the morning. I do not want your ex coming back there tonight because I need the place to be clean when we leave. Please do not come into my room to say goodbye when you get back. Consider this our goodbye." And indeed that was the last time I saw Gabby.

Eventually, I sent Gabby a text message telling her how much her behavior had hurt me and that I was walking away from both the money she owed me and from our friendship. Then I blocked her to ensure I had a clean break.

Bestie, relationships are like bank accounts. You are investing the precious resources of your time, love, and effort. Giving any amount of these resources represents a withdrawal from your emotional bank account. While that might sound cold, it's not; you're spending this currency on your friends and loved ones because you care, because you *want* to. But just like you shouldn't overdraft your actual bank account, you shouldn't keep swiping your emotional debit card without replenishing it.

If there is someone in your life who only registers withdrawals and never deposits, someone who has you on the verge of emotional bankruptcy, it might be time to decide whether they deserve a place in your life. Relationships—the good ones, anyway—work both ways. And, Bestie, you *deserve* that.

For a long time, I had held on to the idea of Gabby. But once I had the epiphany that I was literally putting myself in harm's way (through the temptation to drink, getting into a car with drunk drivers, or who knows what else) by being around her, I realized I *never* wanted to be that person again. I knew that our friendship didn't align with who I was trying to become. I had promised to show up for myself and be my own bestie. To do that, I had to let go of Gabby and the idea that I needed someone else to take care of me.

To this day, I truly believe my experience in New Orleans had a huge impact on my long-term success in sobriety and healing.

Releasing our friendship allowed me to feel a new sense of confidence rooted in the deep knowledge that I had protected my heart, my health, and my peace. Once upon a time, I had felt like I needed someone else to protect me; now I could protect myself. So . . . thanks to Gabby's ex, I guess?

I know it's not easy to end a friendship, even at the point when you realize that the other person is taking more than they're giving, that your evolving boundaries don't allow for the friendship anymore, or for any other reason. There's no way around it: Friendship breakups are roooooough. But no matter how hard it is—no matter how sad or afraid or anything else you feel about the idea of ending a friendship that no longer serves you—the friend you owe the most to is yourself. Bringing a friendship that no longer works to an end is an important way of affirming that your needs matter. That *you* matter.

So here's what I want you to do, my sweet, kind, endlessly generous Bestie: Take a look at the relationships in your life. Ask yourself if they are balanced. Is the love you give being reciprocated in kind? Let's see what this looks like.

1. Map Out Your Circle—I want you to make a list of the people you spend most of your time with and give the most emotional energy to. This includes friends, family, co-workers, your weird uncle you couldn't wear shorts around, even your neighborhood barista if you have a caffeine addiction.

2. Reflect on the Balance—For each person I want you to ask yourself:

    - Do I feel safe, seen, and valued around them?
    - Am I giving more than I'm receiving?

- Do I feel drained, dismissed, or disrespected after spending time with them?
- Have they been supportive of the changes I have been making?

  Highlight any relationships where the answers feel unbalanced. Be honest, no sugarcoating it just because you go way back.

3. Define Your Boundaries—Go to those highlighted relationships and write out what a healthy boundary would look like. Is it avoiding talking about certain topics? Spending less time together? Or being clear that you will no longer participate in bad habits? Then I want you to practice setting that boundary with them. You can do it in your journal, in the mirror, wherever you need, and then in real life when you're ready.
4. Reassess and Realign—Check in regularly. Have *you* honored your boundary? Have they? Also, how do you feel since shifting the dynamic? If a relationship no longer supports your growth, you're allowed to let it go. It doesn't make you a bad person, it makes you a brave one.

So set boundaries, protect your peace, and don't be afraid to let go of the people in your life who are overdrafting your emotional bank account. Because you are worth so much more than spare change.

“

You can still be a good person while telling someone who is disrespecting you to fuck off.

CHAPTER 8

LESS BITTER, MORE GLITTER

When I was a young kid still trying to figure out who I was, I learned that music was not only a talent of mine but also something that fueled my fire and brought me joy. Bestie, I wasn't good at music; I was *exceptional.* I could sing, I could pick up an instrument and teach myself to play it within a few weeks, and I wasn't shy about sharing this part of me with anyone and everyone—for a while, at least. But as it turned out, the very kids I wanted to be friends with—the ones who also loved the performing arts—didn't appreciate my innate abilities. This was especially true of the only other gay kid in my class (and all of my town, for that matter); he *really* hated it. But I wanted these kids to be my friends, and I knew that standing out because of my big talent and the big joy it brought me wasn't helping my cause. I believed that I needed to be accepted and validated by everyone. So I shrunk down and let other people shine in hopes they wouldn't hate me.

This need of mine to be liked was so strong that in hindsight, I can see how it was not only a major contributor to my lack of self-esteem but also fed into my alcoholism. I was stuck in a vicious cycle of worrying too much about what other people thought about me and then beating myself up for not giving 100 percent when an opportunity presented itself. I was perpetually walking on a tightrope: How much of my authentic self could I let out while still being liked by the people around me?

Leap forward to the end of 2019, where many months into my sobriety, I found myself back in rehearsals for yet another cruise ship. I had decided it was going to be my final cruise and was using it as an opportunity to save money so that I could move to London and reinvigorate my theatre dreams across the pond. For once, I went into the contract happy and hopeful.

The cast for this cruise was very small—just four singers and two dancers. I had only met the other performers in passing before, with one exception: the other male singer, Mateo.

Mateo and I had done a cruise together a couple of years before. He was an incredible, passionate singer, very funny, and a big ball of energy. The only problem with Mateo was that he didn't like me. It didn't start that way, and the baffling part was that I couldn't pinpoint where the fracture in our friendship even occurred.

We had been fine and then, suddenly, Mateo just didn't seem to like me. But, then again, I was still drinking at the time and, to be honest, didn't particularly like myself either, which certainly hadn't helped our relationship. Basically, my general feeling was that between us it was like I'm rubber and you're glue, whatever you say bounces off me and sticks to you. You know, real mature stuff.

But I had spent the past several months growing and healing myself, and I wanted this last cruise to be a happy one. So when I arrived at the house where the cast was all staying for a few weeks during rehearsal, I greeted Mateo just as enthusiastically as I greeted everyone else. On our first night there, the two of us found a moment to chat and had a great heart-to-heart conversation about letting our past go. It appeared that we both wanted to make a fresh start out of this adventure we were about to embark on. *Perfect!* I thought. *This is exactly what I hoped for.*

As we hopped right into the rigorous schedule of rehearsals, everything seemed to be going okay. Being a perfectionist and a professional, I was very focused on learning the material for the shows. Mateo and I weren't *best* friends, but we were getting along.

One morning a few weeks into rehearsal, per usual I woke up and made myself a cup of coffee. I had a headache, so instead of drinking it in the bright, sun-soaked kitchen like I usually did, I decided to enjoy my coffee in the living room, where the curtains were drawn and the room was dark. There I sat, sipping my coffee as the others got their morning started.

"Where's Misha?" I heard one of the girls ask in the kitchen.

"He's not here. He must have gone to the gym," Mateo replied. From there, he continued to say how relieved he was that I wasn't there because he couldn't stand to look at my face anymore.

I listened as the three of them complained and gossiped about me, mostly led by Mateo, who was trying to convince them that I was a bad person. I didn't hear any specifics about what I had done to incite these feelings, just a vague harshness toward me.

Bestie, I might cuss like a sailor and have a strong backbone that allows me to stand up against bullies, but I'm actually a very sensitive person. Hearing the people I was spending the next six months with—and who I thought I was building friendships with—giggle and sneer at my expense truly hurt my feelings.

The old Misha would have lashed out and caused a big scene, giving them an actual reason to hate me. But this new version of me was trying not to be so impulsive. I didn't want to simply react to my feelings; I wanted to feel and process them. So despite my heartache, I mustered up the courage to walk around the corner, silently place my coffee mug in the sink, then walk to my bedroom and shut the door. Suddenly, I felt very alone.

Later that day I spoke to the girls about what had happened. They were apologetic and said that the combination of stress about work and Mateo being in their ear made them just kind of go along with it. Our conversation didn't make everything better, but it did allow me to remain hopeful that this would be a one-time thing.

When the time presented itself, I pulled Mateo aside and told him that I had meant what I said about wanting this contract to be a fresh start for the two of us. I told him that I didn't understand what I had done to deserve his hostility and that I didn't appreciate him drawing the rest of the cast into the drama. Despite my better judgment, I believed Mateo when he apologized and explained that he'd been feeling grumpy and had taken it out on me. "It won't happen again," he assured me.

Except it *did* happen again. In fact, it happened over and over again before we even got on the ship, and it continued to happen after we set sail. Mateo threw a tantrum every few weeks, usually because he overheard someone compliment my performance or because he seemed to feel I was getting too much attention.

In the wake of the tantrums, I always found myself ostracized by the entire cast. I'd feel these awful urges to lash out because my hurt shouldn't have gone unnoticed—but I fought each urge back because I didn't want to sacrifice all the work I'd done on myself. Instead, I swallowed my feelings while the others got ready for shows together, ate meals together, explored whatever port we were in together, and spent most nights hanging out in one of their cabins to watch a film or have some drinks. Not once was I invited, even when I hinted that I didn't have plans. But even during the more peaceful times, I was constantly walking around on eggshells and felt very isolated.

I tried, Bestie, I really tried. But there was no escaping this floating world of a small-town high school in the middle of the Caribbean Sea.

There was one day in particular that felt like emotional whiplash. That morning I was super shocked when Mateo came to my cabin door. He knew that I was friends with a doctor who offered Botox to fellow crew members for a discount, and Mateo wanted to know what the experience was like. Feeling that familiar desire to be liked, I allowed myself to latch on to Mateo's lucid and friendly demeanor. I not only told him about the Botox but also offered to accompany him while he got it done.

We spent the entire day together. First, we went to the spa, and then we decided to get some lunch, followed by coffee and a chat by the pool. It felt like the kind of bonding day that I had always wanted but had never had the opportunity to enjoy, and I was left with the feeling that something had shifted for the better.

That night we had a show, which included a humorous duet between me and Mateo. This song normally felt awkward to perform because of our strained relationship, but tonight we were having more fun with it. The shift was real!

After the show, we left the stage and went to the theatre doors to de-greet guests as they filed out. Mateo and I were standing next to each other, receiving all the standard compliments: "Where do you get all of your energy?" "Best show I've ever seen on a ship!" "You kids ever think about becoming professionals?"

But then a guy walked up to me and said, "Your rendition of Mr. Bojangles was the best I've ever heard! You're just as good or better than any performer I've seen on Broadway." Then he turned to Mateo and said, "You were *so* sweaty up there!" Diabolical. (And true!) But I can understand that hearing someone else get a very high compliment and then being told that you looked like a drowned rat onstage probably doesn't feel great.

When we got back to the dressing rooms, I asked Mateo and another dancer what their plans were. Without even looking at me, Mateo replied, "Don't fucking talk to me." And just like that, any progress we'd made vanished.

One night soon after, I spent hours at the crew bar talking about how much I hated Mateo. Normally, I use my sharp tongue to defend myself or someone else who is on the receiving end of some shit stain bully, but this time I was the offender. I was being mean and I knew it—not only because I felt it, but also because the people I was talking to were clearly uncomfortable and just wanted to enjoy their night after a hard day's work. I went back to my cabin feeling embarrassed about how I had acted. Up until this point in my newfound sobriety, I had worked hard to maintain a level head, but the inescapable weight of this social catastrophe was threatening to demolish the foundation I had worked so hard to establish.

I thought back to Little Misha and the times during my childhood when I had dimmed my light so as not to outshine the people around me who I could sense felt jealous. Music and performing are practically synonymous with who I am, so I never stopped doing what I loved. But it did make me hyper-fixate on not allowing myself to feel too proud or too confident in myself. It stole a lot of the joy out of what should have filled up my soul. This turned into bitterness and resentment. My otherwise glittery self didn't sparkle as bright.

Once I noticed this pattern repeating itself on the ship, I decided I would be damned if I dulled my own shine for the sake of being accepted again. And I also didn't want to be bitter or petty in reaction to my own hurt. I was going to perform without worrying about other people's feelings, and I wasn't going to turn into a nasty person just because I couldn't manage someone else's emotions.

So, awkward as it was to get onstage with people who clearly wished I'd jump overboard, from then on, I made a conscious decision to go out there and shine as brightly as I could every single day—not only onstage but offstage as well. If I was going to be on this ship, and *especially* if this was going to be the last contract I ever did at sea, I was going to give it my all.

This obviously didn't help my situation with Mateo since he grew nastier with every compliment that came my way, but it *did* allow me to get to know other crew members onboard who stopped to give me a compliment in the crew areas after they saw the show. Eventually, I started to make a group of friends outside of the cast.

Even after I started to branch out, I still occasionally spent a day out with the cast, as social mores required. On one of those occasions, I texted the group chat to ask what the plan was for the day. Crickets. I could see that they had all read my message, but not a single one of them responded. Eventually I got off the ship by myself and went to a beach club where we had hung out a few times before. They were all there when I arrived, sitting at a table and laughing.

It felt like one of those scenes in a movie where the unpopular kid sees the cool kids hanging out. But I refused to slink away. Every eye roll, every solitary evening in my cabin, every single second I had put Mateo's ego ahead of my feelings had finally boiled over. I instantaneously stopped caring about what *they* wanted and became interested only in what *I* needed. I walked my talented little ass over to that table, stood tall at the head of it, and said, "Hey, guys, I'm done trying to get you to like me. We don't have to have any sort of relationship outside of work. It's a shame because, Mateo, I think your insecurities have become a cancer to this cast and made these girls act in nasty ways that they probably wouldn't have otherwise. Also . . . fuck you."

With that, I turned and walked away. Bestie, as soon as the adrenaline left my body all I could feel was *relief*. Until that moment, I don't think I fully realized just how sad being excluded had made me feel. And now I felt relief because I knew that I had just taken action to protect my joy. To care for and support myself, just like I would if a friend of mine was being bullied. Immediately, I felt a spring in my step. Something in me came back to life.

Over the next few weeks, I stuck to my word. I focused on work, my friends from other departments, and refused to give an ounce of my energy to these people who had made me feel like shit. The strange part was how they were now trying to change my mind. It was as if my lack of desperation for their approval and pleading with them to like me was a huge blow to their collective singular-brain-celled ego.

A few nights later, there was a knock on my cabin door. I opened it to find Mateo standing there, in all of his five foot, five inches of glory. "Can we talk?" he asked.

When I nodded and let him in, Mateo pulled a piece of paper out of his pocket, saying that he'd written a letter to read to me because he was nervous. In it, he wrote that he was sorry for treating me the way he had. He admitted that I hadn't done anything to warrant his behavior; he was just very insecure and I intimidated him. He explained that anytime I got a compliment he felt untalented, that my ambition to perform beyond the ship made him feel like he was wasting his time, and that he generally had a hard time building healthy relationships with men.

Look, Bestie, I can feel empathy for the fact that Mateo had deep insecurities that likely stemmed from childhood. *Hi! I've been there.* But that didn't mean I had to be his punching bag, his therapist, or his friend. I let Mateo finish his letter and thanked him for his apology. But we had been here before. I meant it when I said I was done.

And, bitch! As it turns out, I was right to feel that way because not even two weeks later Mateo had a nuclear meltdown over the same silly things that had triggered him in the past. But this time it didn't even faze me. I had realized that life was a lot more enjoyable when I chose my own happiness over validation from people who needed to be persuaded to like me.

You might not even realize you're doing it, but by working on yourself, growing your confidence, and claiming the life you want, you are building an unshakable foundation for yourself. Which is huge, because it means that when life inevitably throws some shit your way, that bedrock will allow you to stand strong. If you've done the work, you get to keep your joy, even in the face of adversity, pain, and ugly men with dating podcasts. Who wants to be a bitter old queen, Bestie? Not you.

But before we move on, I have to share the funny and ironic ending to this chapter of my life. That particular Stephen King–level nightmare of a contract happened to be underway as COVID started, though we crew members were none the wiser because we lived in the little bubble of the ship. We had no idea that COVID was even a thing until the captain pulled us into a meeting and informed us that all the passengers were disembarking that very day because of a worldwide health concern. He also told us that the crew was going to sail out to sea for the next 30 days to wait out COVID without any guests onboard, and we would not be allowed off the ship for any reason during that time.

The moment the meeting ended I pranced my way directly to HR and told them that I was getting off the ship immediately and would buy my own plane ticket home. I knew without a doubt that it was time for me to let go of this situation, these people, and the baggage we had collectively created. I needed to affirm for myself that it was okay to choose my peace and joy rather than continuing to wade through a situation that just didn't feel good. As I towed my suitcases to the gangway, the relief I felt was palpable.

In the moments when I had felt the worst on that ship, I allowed forces outside of myself to knock me off track and distract me from being the person I wanted to be. I couldn't change my situation until I got off the boat—but I *could* change my choices and how I chose to react. I could decide to take power into my own hands rather than giving it to someone else.

Now it's time for you to take an honest look inward: Are there situations in your life that you're allowing to knock you off track or draw you away from the person you want to be? If so, have you considered the fact that you can make a different choice? That you can choose glitter over bitter?

Here's a guide to helping you avoid losing yourself to the opinions of other people:

- Spot the Sparkle Thieves—I want you to think of the moments where you inarguably feel like *you*. When you are shining, confident, and lit up from the inside out. And now I want you to write down who didn't clap. Who rolled their eyes, or changed the subject, or made you feel like you were too much. This isn't about blame; it's clarity, babe.

- Recognize the Shift—Next, I want you to write about how you reacted. Did you shrink? Did their lack of enthusiasm make you second-guess yourself or turn yourself into a version of you that you're not proud of? Be honest.

- Rewrite the Scene—Here's where the glow-up happens. Go back to that same situation, but this time, you don't let the bitch get you down. You don't get bitter; you don't get petty. You get glittery. How can you show up and protect your sparkle without losing your softness?

- Lock It In with an Affirmation—Reaffirm yourself with a go-to mantra. Mine is, "My joy is sacred. I don't shrink, I shine." Write it down on a Post-it note and slap it on your mirror, Bestie.

Too often we allow people and things that really aren't that important in the grand scheme of things to hold power over us. It's easy to get sucked into the drama. It can feel tempting to tone yourself down or give in to the urge to retaliate. But by categorically denying these people and situations access to your time and instead focusing your energy on your own joy, you can cut the rope of the anchor that's pulling you down into the depths of unhappiness.

Come up for air, Bestie—you deserve it.

“You might not even realize you’re doing it, but by working on yourself, growing your confidence, and claiming the life you want, you are building an unshakable foundation for yourself.”

CHAPTER 9

LIVE, LAUGH, LOVE YOURSELF

Hey, Bestie! As world-famous drag queen RuPaul says, "If you can't love yourself, how in the hell can you love somebody else? Can I get an amen?" I have always loved that tagline because I've been shouting a similar sentiment at every opportunity I get ever since I felt the cosmic shift of loving myself. The joy and abundance you feel when you realize that you've always had the power inside of you and you just needed to let it out changes everything.

I know, I know, you're probably thinking, "Okay, bitch. That sounds nice, but how do I do it?" Let's get to it.

I spent so much of my life swimming in insecurity, internalizing any criticism that came my way. I was focused on the things that I felt were keeping me small—until I decided to let all of that crap go and affirm myself. Today I can see myself clearly, and my sense of worth doesn't come from how other people perceive me. Once I made that choice, all those insecurities that used to drive my life suddenly became *funny*. And I have to tell you: Funny is freedom.

A good example of this is when I get nasty comments about my teeth on social media. (First of all, bitch, my upper teeth are nearly perfect, and, yes, my bottom teeth have some personality, but I actually get quite a few comments from people saying they're "obsessed" with them.) When my teeth get trolled, I often respond with a comment like, "I may have teeth that look like a haunted piano, but at least I don't have summer teeth like you. Some are there, some aren't." The people who leave these comments *think* they're funny while hurting me at the same time. But my superpower is I will just out-funny them. Every time.

I've found that there's a lot of power in responses like this that take the criticism intended to hurt me and dull its blade. *And* it makes me laugh in the process, which just feels good. It certainly feels better than marinating in the meaningless negativity some basement dweller is throwing my way.

Every time I alchemize something that was supposed to be hurtful into humor, I think of my friend Billy, who taught me about the power of humor. I met Billy doing my first Cirque tour. Yes, I performed with Cirque du Soleil as a singer, and Billy was a professional jump-roper. Nope, I didn't know that was a thing before joining the circus either.

Not only was Billy an incredible athlete, but he was brimming with charisma and personality. He had worked with Cirque for many years, and on top of jump-roping, he was also a clown in the show. He had a few scenes where he conducted the audience in a group participation activity, and those were always a huge hit. Without saying a word, Billy could make thousands of people laugh.

Billy and I became fast friends. We bonded over our shared love of our lord and savior, Britney Spears, and fed off each other's life-of-the-party personality. He had enormous dreams that extended far beyond what we were currently doing, and I spent many nights in hotel rooms listening as Billy ruminated on them. When the two of us were together, we were like a tornado of snarky commentary, bad influence, and lots and lots of laughter.

We also shared some less-than-glamorous qualities. Like me, Billy had his own insecurities. One of Billy's biggest insecurities was his body. Relatable, right?

Billy was a full-blooded Alabama-bred man. He often joked, "I look more like the guy who drives the tour bus than a performer in the show." And I understood why he felt that way. All the other acrobats had a combined body fat percentage less than the number of calories in a stick of sugar-free gum. While the Russians survived on boiled chicken, broccoli, and push-ups, Billy enjoyed coming out with me to destroy some chicken wings and wash them down with enough beer to put an adult gorilla to sleep.

Needless to say, he didn't have six-pack abs or a body that didn't jiggle, but that didn't stop him from getting into spandex costumes and doing the same stunts as the rest of the cast, even though he knew that he would get comments from the audience at the stage door like, "I thought you were in a fat suit to make it funny!" or, "You're very talented, but maybe you could get some workout tips from the other performers." Those were actual things people had the audacity to say to his face. It must have been hard to go out there in front of thousands of people and pour your heart out, only to be thinking about how they are looking at the size of your body instead of the size of your talent.

And this wasn't an experience that Billy faced solely at work. Being a bigger guy in the gay community is ruthless. If you aren't a skinny little thing with abs or a muscly hunk with abs, then you don't really get let into the club. Abs are literally the entrance fee.

Billy was always talking about how he wanted to have a fairy-tale romance. But I never saw him put himself out there to find someone to love him in that way. He mostly allowed himself cheap and fast encounters with people only interested in sex, because that way he protected his heart against rejection.

But despite feeling some frustration and wanting more out of life, both personally and professionally, Billy almost never let it show on the outside. He had this rare magic about him that made people love him instantly.

Billy's superpower was his ability to bring out the best in the people around him. I know he did that for me. He didn't just light up a room, he turned on everyone else's light too. There was this one time we ended up in a dive bar in a tiny town in Arizona. Imagine the type of people who would frequent a hole-in-the-wall biker bar, just minding their own business when, all of a sudden, a group of Russian acrobats, Mongolian contortionists, and a bunch of gays come crashing in.

You know in the movies when a character who isn't supposed to be somewhere walks in the door and the record scratches as everyone turns to look at them? That literally happened! It was super uncomfortable. That is, until Billy said, "Hey, folks! We look weird because we're in the circus, and we stopped in your town on our way to Phoenix. But please don't beat us up. We're here to *party*!" It turned out to be one of the funnest nights on the entire tour. But, then again, every night with Billy was fun because he was such a magnetic force of nature, with so much It Factor that he was easily the most popular person in any and every room.

Then there was the most random and fun night I ever had in New York City, mostly thanks to Billy. I had won a lottery for tickets to see an all-female version of *Taming of the Shrew* at the Shakespeare in the Park series that plays in Central Park every summer, which I was very excited about because I had never been to Shakespeare in the Park and had recently played the role of Tranio in another production of *Taming of the Shrew*. Billy was always a "yes" guy, so I asked him to join me and, not surprisingly, he didn't disappoint.

Billy and I met up at a little gay bar in midtown Manhattan that we frequented when we wanted to cause trouble and dance the night away. After a few vodka sodas, we headed toward Central Park. Imagine two very flamboyant and very obviously tipsy gays prancing down the streets of NYC in broad daylight. We were a sight.

At a certain point along our journey toward this culturally elitist evening, Billy stopped dead in his tracks. "Wait!" he said, as if he was the star of a really cheesy Disney show and had just thought of a brilliant plan. "Should we get some wine to sneak in with us so we don't have to pay eighteen dollars for some shitty house red in a plastic cup?"

Obviously, there's only one answer to this question, and that answer is: *fuck, yes*.

Billy and I made a pit stop, bought a bottle of red wine and two large bottles of water (which we poured out and replaced with the wine), and continued making our way to the show. When we got to the entrance, security was very clearly checking bags for contraband, so Billy took the water bottle filled with wine out of my hand and shoved both of our bottles into the front of his pants. He looked at me with a devilish grin and a little wink.

Such a simple plan, but that didn't stop both of us from thinking that Billy was an evil genius mastermind. We got through the security checkpoint with no problem—because, honestly, those people don't make enough money to care about two homos who want to save a few bucks—and went on to gleefully watch the show. (Sidebar: it was incredible.)

After the show ended and everyone from Central Park was crowding the already-busy Manhattan streets, Billy did what he did best: He made a new friend. We were standing on a corner, trying to figure out which way we wanted to go, when Billy noticed another gay guy who was wearing the flashiest of outfits. Billy complimented his style and struck up a conversation with him; within two minutes we were invited to a private party at a gay bar in the West Village.

This is the point where we found ourselves in a conundrum. It was way too early to be going to a club, but not early enough that it made sense to go to either of our apartments, since we both lived in the opposite direction of the club. After pondering our best strategy for a moment, Billy suggested that we walk from midtown to the West Village and stop at any bars that spoke to us along the way.

Off we went. We stopped in one iconic bar at the bottom of Hell's Kitchen, where you get a free hot dog with every drink purchased, figuring that would make for a good dinner. By the time we got to the club, we were more inebriated than we had any business being while around the general population. Nevertheless, we walked up to the door we were told to go to. The bouncer took one look at us in our underwhelming theatre-in-the-park attire and said, "Sorry. This is a private event."

My first thought was that we had been duped. I figured there was no way we were getting in and that we had just walked all the way here for nothing. But Billy just laughed and replied, "Oh, you misunderstand. We're on the list." And what do you know? We were, indeed, on the list.

We entered the dark club, catching glimpses of the room and the people occupying it only when the strobe lights intermittently flashed. For as drunk as I was, I remember thinking, *How did I go from watching Shakespeare, to touring dive bars of New York City, to an underground gay nightclub?*

I felt totally out of place. Everyone else was dressed in the most audacious outfits: huge platform shoes, copious amounts of leather, and, in some cases, very little clothing at all. If you know anything about the Club Kids of New York City from the 1980s and '90s, this was the vibe. In fact, trans icon Amanda Lepore was there that very night.

But you know who did *not* feel out of place? Billy. The tiny, smoke-filled room was packed with skinny gays showing their six-pack abs, but Billy was right there in the middle of the dance floor having the time of his life. His aura shined brighter than the disco ball spinning above his head. I remember looking at him and thinking it must be so freeing to have that kind of confidence—a confidence that I didn't have in a room full of strangers. We stayed at the party until the alcohol caught up to us and told us it was time to go home. It was one of many fun and unexpected nights with my friend.

A couple of years ago, I was sitting on my couch when I received a text from Billy. "I need your help," it read. There wasn't any context, but I didn't need any—I would always be happy to help Billy, whatever he needed.

"Sure thing," I responded. "What's up?" I assumed he had a general question or maybe wanted some advice choosing an outfit for the night.

But Billy never responded. That was the last I ever heard from my friend Billy. A few short months later I found out that he had passed away.

I had a hard time making sense of the news that Billy had died. He filled the world with such a special and unique quality of light and joy; he wasn't supposed to leave us. I read the comments from hundreds of people online, expressing their grief, and also celebrating how positively and how powerfully he had changed their lives.

As I was celebrating my fifth anniversary of being sober on Christmas Day 2023, I picked up my phone and wished so badly that I could text Billy. "I did it!" I would write. I knew he would understand the gravity of this milestone in ways that a lot of my other friends and family just couldn't.

I had learned so much from Billy's ability to laugh at his own insecurities before the world could. He wasn't going to be defined by the perceptions of others—he was going to define himself. Although he left this world, he didn't leave it quietly. In his wake was a shitstorm of sadness, disbelief, and also lovely memories forever ingrained in people's minds—the kind of memories that only Billy could create.

As I was sitting down and planning this book, I knew that I wanted to include a chapter about not letting our insecurities become the thing that defines us. I wanted to express the ways in which we can take that power back and make it work in our favor, rather than allowing it to paralyze us. But I had no idea how I was going to get the point across. Literally, as I sat there thinking, "Bitch! Is this writer's block?" the song "Toxic," by none other than Britney Spears, came on. I laughed so hard that I started crying.

So, to Billy: I love you so much. I miss you so much. I still find myself stuck somewhere between grieving and celebrating your life. Thank you for sending me that message from Britney. You inspired me so much over the years, and now you get to continue to impact the world through this book. It's Billy, bitch.

Now it is your turn. I want you to channel Billy too, Bestie. I want you to reclaim some of that power back that you may have given up because of insecurities. Here's what I want you to do:

- Recognize the Insecurity—Grab your journal and write down something that you are insecure about. Start with just one, the one that shows up when you walk into a room or meet someone for the first time. What do you tell yourself about it? What do you think others are thinking?
- Become a Stand-Up Comedian—Flip the script, Bestie. Try thinking of all the ways you or someone else has insulted that insecurity and try to make it funnier. Take away that motherfucker's power.
- Rewrite the Narrative—Billy let doors remain open for him despite his insecurities because he winked at them instead of hiding from them. If you walk into the same kind of room or meet a new person, how do you move differently, speak differently? Who gets drawn to you because you're too busy laughing to remember that bitch-ass voice in your head even exists?

Most people are so caught up in their own shit that they aren't noticing nearly as much about you as you think they are.

The next time you are feeling trapped in a cycle of judging or even hating things about yourself, do what Britney does on social media and just spin around a lot. Or better yet, do what Billy would do and pour some wine into an empty water bottle and go have an adventure. Have fun with it and remember, you're a lot—ahem, *stronger*—than you think you are.

Can I get an amen?

“Most people are so caught up in their own shit that they aren’t noticing nearly as much about you as you think they are.”

CHAPTER 10

CLAP BACK CONFIDENCE

Hey, Bestie! You have arrived at what is, in my opinion, the most fun part of this transformational journey we're on together: letting the world *have it* if they don't jump on board with your fabulous new self. Let the world eat your damn shorts if they try to pull you back down to their level. Or fire away and let them have it when they're just plain ol' being an asshole.

I can't think of a better way to demonstrate what I'm talking about than by sharing some of my most popular social media stories involving clapbacks. Because, not to brag, but I'm *kind of* amazing at clapping back—although, let me be clear, I wasn't always. Standing up against bullies requires a lot of confidence. A bully will smell your fear like a vulture circling roadkill, and they will come at you even harder if you aren't ready for them. But I have found that most of these terrible people are also acting out of their own insecurities and traumas. The more confident you are, the more it intimidates them.

Your clapbacks don't have to sound like mine, but what *is* important is that you understand that defending yourself—and others, when need be—is not only okay, but a crucial part of protecting that confidence you're building up. And yes, it can take some practice, but I *also* encourage you to have fun with it because watching some idiot who doesn't realize that they're what's ugly in this world being forced to look in a mirror is priceless.

Whether you've already heard these stories online and are reliving them here or are being introduced to my lethal tongue for the first time, I want you to know that I *do* think it's important to treat others with a baseline of respect and understanding. But if others can't find it in themselves to treat you with that same baseline of respect and understanding . . . well, whatever happens to their feelings and ego as a result of their own choices is none of your damn business.

The first story I want to share took place in the cultural hellscape that is Sephora. But, no, this story doesn't involve a hormonal tween screaming at her mother to buy her a $239 bottle of face cream. This is a story about an occasion where I was confronted by an Older Lady Who Can't Mind Her Own Business.

Not only do I create social media, but I also consume it, and some of my favorite videos are makeup reviews and tutorials. These videos inspired me to play with makeup myself, which leads me to Sephora. On this particular day, I went in to buy some foundation. New to makeup at the time, I decided to ask an employee to color match me with the perfect shade for my skin tone. I was a pretty confident bitch by that point, so I would have been comfortable asking anyone for help with this mission, but I was still pleased to see a guy who worked there with a full face of glam makeup. Fun!

This guy was just as helpful as I'd hoped. He asked me about the results I was looking for, what I had already tried, and then proceeded to match me with the right shade. As we were minding our own business, living our best lives, I noticed this old bitch looking at us with the same look I imagine she has when she pulls her husband's dirty tighty-whities out of the hamper. I mean, she was *disgusted*. But I was in a good mood that day so, like Elsa, I was going to let it go.

But she continued to stand there, shamelessly glaring at me. Eventually, I turned to her and asked, "Is there something you would like to say to me?"

Most normal people would feel horrified to be called out for staring at a stranger, but nope! Not this lady. She clutched her collar and said, "You're disgusting." Can you *believe*!?

"Your face looks like a crinkle-cut French fry," I replied. "There isn't a damn thing in this store that will help you, you dial-up Internet, home phone, cable TV, Facebook-using, Ask Jeeves–looking bitch!"

This woman gaped at me like I had just slapped her dead mom. Like *I* did something wrong. Do you know how often this happens? Someone shows their whole ass and then, when confronted with some wind blowing up their business, they act like the wind is the problem. I find it infuriating when a person plays the victim when they were, in fact, just victimizing someone else.

I lowered my tone and told this granny to mind her own business and leave us alone. But instead of taking her Jurassic ass to Mickey D's to buy a Filet-O-Fish, she decided to regurgitate the same boring-ass comeback that's been recited by homophobes for years. "We're tired of you guys shoving your lifestyle down our throats." Original!

"Disrespectfully," I replied, "you would know if I shoved something down your throat, but you don't have to worry about that because there's just *something* about tooth decay that turns me off. You look like you have about fourteen days left on this earth, so if I were you, I'd stop wasting that time being bothered by us simply existing."

Was I harsh? *Yes.* I was ruthless. Do I hate older people? *Absolutely not.* But this woman went out of her way to try to make life more uncomfortable for me just because she felt like it. There had been no altercation—and, in fact, no interaction at all—between us. Yet, she felt it was acceptable to attack me for simply existing, so I gave her a taste of her own medicine . . . which is probably Lipitor.

Bestie, if you're thinking, "But, Misha, you don't have to stoop to her level," I have to tell you that I hate that argument. I think it's important to stand up to someone when they believe it's their right to degrade another person because, otherwise, what lesson will they learn? That the person they thought was weak and beneath them is willing to roll over and accept their abuse? Fuck that. My opinion is that a bully who gets back a dose of what they're serving can lick their wounds and think twice about going out of their way to be hateful.

My second story comes to you compliments of a first date—but not mine. One day I went out for lunch at a local café and happened to be seated next to an older couple on a first date. The woman was beautiful and had clearly put in some effort preparing for this lunch. Her hair was done, she was wearing subtle makeup that enhanced her already gorgeous features, and she was very engaged with the man sitting across the table. He, on the other hand, looked like he had *just* learned how to stand up and like his sex life consisted entirely of his right hand reenacting the I-wish-I-knew-how-to-quit-you scene from *Brokeback Mountain*.

I overheard the woman share that she had beaten breast cancer a few years earlier, after having a double mastectomy. Let's pause here, Bestie, because I want you to think about all of the ways you might appropriately respond to a stranger being vulnerable with you like this. Got it? Okay, well, none of your responses are what transpired at the table next to me.

"Well, at least you got some new boobs out of it!" I heard the man say. "They look great!" Did I mention he was staring right at her chest as he said this?

Understandably, this poor woman's entire energy shifted. It was clear to anyone who had a brain that she was upset, but unfortunately, her date seemed oblivious. It was hard to tell whether this man's credit score or IQ were lower.

When the oaf excused himself to go to the bathroom a few minutes later, I glanced over at the woman and saw that she was wiping a tear from her eye. “Are you okay?” I asked gently, leaning toward her. She shook her head and shared that this was the very first date she’d been on since her cancer diagnosis, and she felt like she’d just been punched in the gut. I asked if I could join her for lunch; she nodded and I scooched over into the Neanderthal’s seat.

A couple of moments later, the man came back (with noticeably dry hands for having just used the bathroom, might I add) and looked at me like a caveman who was seeing fire for the first time. “Who are you?” he demanded.

Ignoring his question, I told this guy that he was free to leave because his date deserved to have lunch with a man who would treat her with dignity and respect.

He narrowed his eyes. “I’ll show you a real man!”

I don’t know if he expected me to shrink back, but I certainly didn’t. Instead, I asked if he thought being a man meant making the woman he was on a date with cry. And you know what? He knew *exactly* what I was referring to because he said, “Oh, you mean the titty thing? That was a *joke.*”

His lack of empathy for what this woman had been through infuriated me. “Sir,” I said, “a mastectomy is an *amputation*. Think about that for a minute. Think about the mental toll of having part of your body removed—especially a part of your body that a lot of people associate with womanhood. Not to mention the physical pain and possible lifetime of further procedures afterward.” I paused for a moment. No surprise, this guy had nothing to say for himself in response. “Also,” I continued, “a joke has to be funny. A joke is the fact that eighty percent of your sex life involves being with a lot of lizards from West Texas. A joke is the fact that I bet your parents no longer take your phone calls.”

“My parents are dead,” he retorted, sounding wounded.

"Well," I said, "then they died never knowing what it felt like to be proud of their kid." With that, I waved my hand to dismiss him, and my new friend Eileen and I proceeded to enjoy a wonderful lunch together.

Was I brutally mean to this guy? *Yes.* Do I regret it? *No.* The way I see it, he was comfortable enough in his skin to comment on a woman's body—a woman who had quite literally *just* expressed how insecure she felt—so he got what he deserved. When I shared this story on social media, it received nearly 20 million views across all platforms, and tens of thousands of women commented with their own stories about how breast cancer has affected them.

Think about that for a moment. What does it say that a story about a woman getting mocked by a man caused such a reaction from millions of other women? It's clear to me that too many women have had their own dehumanizing experiences when it comes to their bodies and their health. The vast majority of these same women who at some point felt the blood rush to their faces in embarrassment in response to a man's comments on their body *loved* that I put this dickhead in his place.

The final story I want to share is a lot more serious than the two I've just told. Encountering a rude or judgmental person out in the wild or witnessing someone being a dick on a first date are certainly grounds for standing up for yourself and others. But this last story shows how our confidence can allow us to stand up to someone who is actually dangerous.

One day I was at the pet store getting dog food for my two little assholes. I was holding the largest bag of food I could find while standing in line at the checkout lane. A fully grown man was in front of me—you could tell sheerly by the amount of back hair sticking out of his shirt and the lack of any on his head.

Bestie, I am a Virgo and, like it or not, I am nosy. This man was scrolling social media while he waited, and I could see that literally every single post on his feed was of little girls. Like single-digit ages little. Even more disturbing was the fact that he was zooming in on inappropriate areas of the little girls' bodies and screenshotting them.

"WHAT ARE YOU DOING!?" I shouted as loudly as I could.

Gorilla Back fumbled around and shoved his phone into his pocket like a teenager getting caught with a cigarette. He *knew* what he was doing.

He didn't turn around or acknowledge me in any way so I continued. "IT LOOKED LIKE YOU WERE BEING A PEDOPHILE!"

This man had the fucking audacity to look me in my gay little eyes and say, "We don't actually like that term. It's 'Minor Attracted Person.'"

First of all, *abso-fucking-lutely not*. Second, "we"?! I immediately yelled at the cashier to call someone for help. The man left his cart and ran out of the store.

This is the most viral story I've ever told on social media. Across platforms, it reached more than 30 million views. My comments sections included a discourse about the dangers associated with parents posting photos of their children online. Mommy Bloggers were particularly scrutinized for putting their kids on the Internet for likes and comments when they know these predators are out there, following their accounts and saving photos. It was a really important conversation to have, and many parents sent me messages saying they had deleted all the photos of their children from social media after watching my story.

Here is what I want you to take away from all these stories, Bestie. First and foremost, it is absolutely okay for you to stick up for yourself if someone mistreats you. Giving yourself permission to stand up for yourself when necessary is a way of loving and building yourself up. It's a way of reminding yourself who you are, and that you're worth fighting for.

I've received my fair share of criticism for the way I choose to handle bullies. People often see the world through a very black-and-white lens, and they hate that I don't choose to "be the bigger person" or "let it go." Because that's what we've all been taught, right? But who does that benefit?

It surely doesn't benefit you; after all, I'm not writing this book so you can continue to let people walk all over you. It doesn't benefit other people in the world who can't stand up for themselves but who I happen to have the platform to defend and protect. And it doesn't even benefit the person who needs to be taught a lesson because, believe it or not, the goal of clapping back is to give them an opening to at least consider why they are being called out.

I often think about how so many of us were taught to be "polite" and "nice" to everyone, without question. This is especially true for women. But I categorically reject this. Being a kind person to people who return that same respect and leading any relationship with politeness are certainly the goals. But protecting yourself by removing those restraints when you need to fight back is showing love to yourself.

Imagine if I'd allowed a stranger to degrade me and the employee at Sephora for no other reason than her own hatred. Would she ever have learned a lesson? Would the employee who expresses himself through makeup have thought twice before wearing makeup to work again? I wasn't going to risk it. She wanted to fuck around. She got to find out.

Imagine if I'd done nothing when I saw Eileen sitting there and crying on her date. How long might it have taken for her to put herself out there again? How might she have felt about her own appearance? I think it was worth offending that incredibly thoughtless man if it meant shielding Eileen from feeling like she was worth less because of what she'd been through.

And imagine if I'd looked the other way when I saw a potential child predator out in the wild? *Was* he just saving pictures? Or was he doing (or contemplating) something far worse? I sure don't want to find out. I still think about that incident and hope that the fear of being called out has impacted him in a significant way like by—oh, I don't know—*not* being a fucking pedophile.

I have done the work of telling myself that it's okay to be perceived as a problem as long as I remain aligned with my ethos when calling someone out for bad behavior, and I hope you know it's okay, too, whether your clapbacks sound like mine or not. I want to make the world more fun, more kind, and more safe. There are many ways to do this, and when warranted, clapping back is one of those ways.

And now it's time for you to clap back like a Clapback Queen. The most important thing to remember is that you are confident. Body language is important; make eye contact and stand up straight, with your shoulders pulled back. You should be—or, at least, want to appear—relaxed but assertive.

Next (and this is really important), master the art of the pause. Bullies expect and want you to be flustered. Take a short moment and give them a look that says, *Are you sure?*

And finally, pick the style of clapback that resonates with you most. There is the elegant dismissal: "Bless your heart." Brutal, yet simple. There is the fake concern: "Are you okay? You seem really invested in being an asshole." Or my favorite, the one-liner: "If I wanted to hear from someone irrelevant, I'd check my spam folder."

You know what they say: Practice makes perfect. Believe it or not, you only need one or two good, rehearsed clapbacks to get into the groove of standing up for yourself. If you have a go-to response ready, you can confidently protect yourself, and each time you will be more confident in your reaction. And remember, sometimes the biggest power move you can make is to not react at all. Not everyone is deserving of your time or your words.

I want you to practice in the mirror:

- Body First, Words Later—Stand in front of the mirror with your feet planted, shoulders back, chin up (not too high, this isn't Broadway), and look yourself in the eyes. You are not someone to mess with, you are someone to be respected.
- Practice the Pause—Imagine someone says something batshit to your face. Count one-Mississippi, two-Mississippi . . . and then raise an eyebrow or give a slow blink. That pause? That's power. Think about what it feels like to not jump to explain yourself. You're not defending, you're deciding.
- Choose Your Style—Try out one of the methods we just discussed and keep playing with them until you find a good comeback that sounds like you.
- Know When to Walk Away—Remember that some people don't deserve a comeback. Your silence will bitch-slap them across the face harder than any words you utter to them. Know your worth and protect your peace.

I've said it a million times before, and I will say it again, Bestie: You can tell someone who deserves it to fuck off if they are mistreating you and still be a kind person. You can feel confident in doing so knowing that you are using your power for good. You've done the work, so now the fun begins.

The more
confident
you are,
the more it
intimidates
them.

—Part III—

STAND YOUR GROUND

Now you've self-reflected and affirmed yourself on the journey to looking in the mirror and thinking, "There I am!" Look at you—you're halfway there! Hopefully you've dusted off the bullshit that was weighing you down, found some confidence, and started to treat yourself with some god-dang respect! But now? Well, now it's time we draw some damn boundaries. Because loving yourself isn't just about affirmations. It's about protecting that self-love you're feeling as if it is your most prized possession (because it is). And that means standing your ground.

This is where you stop tolerating less than you deserve. You hear me, Bestie? You need to stop tolerating the users, the energy vampires, and the people who only clap for you when they benefit from your success. You need to refuse to let them take you for granted for even a second longer. This is the time to get to a place where you stop settling or participating in relationships that drain you. It's the moment for you to accept that not everyone is going to like you, and that's *their* problem. Standing your ground isn't about being mean, it's about knowing your worth and refusing to negotiate.

That being said, sometimes the hardest battle isn't with others—it's with yourself. It's time to practice listening to and respecting yourself. This looks like trusting your gut, walking away when something doesn't feel right, and reminding yourself that you are not dramatic for expecting basic respect. That's how you can prove to yourself that you're serious about this whole self-love thing. And here's your power move: *There is always an exit.* If someone—whether it's a friend, a boss, a partner, or even a family member—refuses to respect your boundaries, the door is always there.

So, get ready, because this section is about taking all that power you've built up and actually using it. The stories you're about to read involve discerning when it's time to walk away, when to speak up, and when to let people figure out what they've lost on their own. You've worked so damn hard to become this version of you—and now it's time to protect you at all costs.

CHAPTER 11

MAKE THEM REGRET IT

Hey, Bestie! As the old saying goes, the best revenge is a life well lived. But I've learned the hard way that a lot of people are only happy for you as long as you don't color outside the lines of their self-serving parameters and expectations of you. Once you step even a single toe over that line, that's when their true colors begin to show.

But have you ever thought about this: What would happen if *you* rejected someone else's rejection of you? What if you took all of that self-reflection and the lessons you've learned from it, and all the love you've poured into yourself, and threw it right back in their face by not backing down? Hmmm, it's something to think about.

I can tell you from my own experience that it's possible to take the sadness that often results from suddenly understanding the limits on a particular relationship and transform it into pride. You know how that transformation happens? By standing up for yourself. By letting that person know that you reject the limitations they're placing upon you. Even if that sounds scary, try it out and I bet you'll find that sadness alchemizes into relief and then pride as life continues to show you that you've made the right decision for yourself.

I'll show you what I mean.

After fleeing the ship that Mateo and his gaggle of *Hocus Pocus* witches floated back out to sea on, I rode out the pandemic, like so many of us, by spending more time posting on social media. For me, it was a creative outlet during those weird times when there weren't any performance gigs to be had. Obviously, my plans to move to England couldn't happen (both because of COVID and because I'd met someone worth staying in the U.S. for), so as soon as the world opened up a little more, I started working at a retail job to make ends meet. After one particularly horrid day at work—at a company that, as it turns out, did *not* align with my values—I quit.

I didn't know what I was going to do for money, but I did know that I couldn't continue working there. So I did what anyone would do after marching out those swinging glass doors for the last time: I ran through the mall filming myself shouting, "I QUIT!" and then went home and posted a story about it online.

Well, that video went viral. People from all over the world cheered me on for standing up for what I believed in, and they also shared their own personal experiences about the ways in which this particular brand hadn't been inclusive toward them either. I don't know how to fully describe the whole experience, but the vindication from people who were also fed up with injustice just felt *right*.

Shortly after that, I posted another story about standing up for a young service worker who was being harassed by a customer. That video also blew up, with commenters talking about their own hard days at work, feeling undervalued, or how they wished someone would have stood up for them in similar circumstances.

I had grown into being the same person people were reacting to online—someone who is always willing to stand up for himself, others when necessary, and against the injustices we see every day. The only difference is that now I was out there actually sharing the tales, and it was resonating online in a profound way, gaining me hundreds of thousands of new besties in just a few months.

But as I explored this new and very exciting adventure that was social media, I was still waiting for my old job to become an option again. A producer from my cruise ship job, Bea, told me that she wanted me to be in the first cast back on a ship as soon as they were allowed to resume service. As the vocal captain, I would be in charge of teaching the songs we'd be performing to the other singers and maintaining the integrity of the shows. I know, Bestie—back to a ship! Listen, the pandemic took its toll on me financially, and while social media was popping off, it wasn't paying any bills.

I was ready to sing my heart out to old people sleeping in the front row because they'd drunk too much at dinner. As long as there was money going *into* my bank account rather than out of it, I didn't care how it was getting there.

Originally, I was told I would be leaving to start rehearsals on the ship in two weeks. Then I received an email saying we were delayed for an additional four weeks. And then I didn't hear anything at all for two months. In the end, my ship contract was pushed back by five months, meaning that a year and a half after getting off the last ship, I found myself flying to the Caribbean.

But it was different this time. I had five months of me exploring this new sense of purpose, and also being appreciated online . . . just for being who I am. The entire world was different. *I* was different.

The new post-COVID rules mandated that we ensure no one onboard tested positive, and the crew had to be trained in all the new ways they would have to interact with guests to minimize risk of sickness spreading. The very first thing we had to do was quarantine alone in our respective rooms onboard for 10 days. As you can imagine, Bestie, this was a very long 10 days. To paint a picture for you, a meal was left outside my door three times per day and this was the highlight of my day. But especially after having just spent several months with my husband (who was my boyfriend at the time) and our new dog, Auggie, I felt so lonely.

On the 10th day a doctor knocked on my door and administered a COVID test. A couple hours later I got a call letting me know that my test was negative, and I was *finally* free to leave the luxury prison I had been locked up in. I quickly threw on some clothes and hadn't even pulled up my second sock when my cell phone started to ring. It was my producer, Bea, who was not on the ship.

I answered the phone, expecting her to ask how we were doing, if we needed anything, and to provide instructions about what we should do now that quarantine was over. Instead, I heard Bea's voice bellowing, "CAN YOU EXPLAIN TO ME WHY YOU'VE BEEN ON THAT SHIP FOR TEN DAYS AND I HAVEN'T HEARD A SINGLE UPDATE FROM YOU?"

I was completely taken aback. Bea had never yelled at me before. Calmly, I let her know that I had *just* been released from quarantine literally two minutes ago. I hadn't even *met* the other singers yet, much less worked with them!

Bea continued to scold me for my lack of professionalism and went on about how "disappointed" she was in me. Had this happened a year-and-a-half earlier, I would have been mortified and tripping over myself to apologize. But that was then and this was now. So instead I said, "Okay, did you want me to send you an email every time I wiped my ass?"

Bea did not find this response as amusing as I did. But we *did* end up coming to an understanding that there was a lot of pressure in this newly post-COVID world for this contract to go smoothly. Still, we could have avoided all the drama if Bea had been clear about her need for ongoing communication up front.

Bea was radio silent as the cast and I learned the shows over the next few weeks. She never checked in to see if we were okay; instead, she just left us to figure it out. So much for communication, I guess? Meanwhile, we were having a grand old time hanging out with the crew after we were done rehearsing every day. It truly felt like we were a little family. But that fairy tale didn't last long.

One night, two of the guys from the housekeeping department came over to the table where the entertainment staff was sitting, wondering if we would be willing to ask the event staff if we could have an onboard Pride party since it was June. These guys were from Indonesia and explained that being gay was looked down upon there, so they'd never had the opportunity to go to a Pride party before. Because of their background, they also didn't feel comfortable pitching the idea but figured us entertainers might.

Bestie, you know I love throwing a party, so I was *in*. The entire cast and I went to the next events meeting and presented the idea. The team was immediately all in and started discussing plans for the bar, restaurant, and entertainment teams to do their thing. So amazing, right?

Then the following day we received notice that a "higher up" onboard the ship had shot down the idea of a Pride party because, "It would make men uncomfortable." The men's body odor made me uncomfortable, but you didn't see me trying to ban them from existing. We were all disappointed but just kind of accepted the news. It wasn't exactly unusual. I hate to break it to you, but ships are riddled with homophobia, sexism, cheating, and alcoholism. They're like that messy girl at the bar who you know will be a good time but will also *for sure* throw up in your car later.

At lunch that day, I broke the news to the two guys who had initially asked us to throw the party. I watched as their shoulders fell. It was clear they took the defeat to mean exactly what it was intended to mean: that they didn't deserve to feel pride.

I felt torn between my desire to be a professional team player and the fact that I thought this fucking sucked. Later that night I was in my cabin, growing more and more angry about the decision when the post-quarantine conversation I'd had with Bea popped into my head. That memory was like pouring gasoline onto an already-burning bag of shit. Why was I so concerned with impressing people who didn't seem to care about me or my well-being?

I hopped up, grabbed my phone, and started recording. I made a video explaining what was happening on our ship and why the party was canceled. I directly asked the cruise ship company, who had put rainbow banners on their social media profiles for the month of June, whether they really believed in inclusion or if they only accepted their LGBTQ staff under the condition we do our work, keep our heads down, and shut the fuck up.

I woke up the next morning to a text from Bea that read, "Call me IMMEDIATELY!" My stomach dropped. I opened up my social media to find that the video I had posted about the ship bringing an end to the Pride party had reached over one million views. Turns out I wasn't the only one who thought these large companies needed to do more than change their profile pictures to show solidarity.

I called Bea, and to my surprise, she told me that she couldn't believe what was happening and stood behind me 100 percent. She also told me a call had been scheduled for later that day with me, the head of HR, the president of the company, and Bea. Of course I felt nervous, but I also knew that the only reason they wanted to speak with me so quickly was for the purposes of damage control. There were already a lot of eyes on the cruise industry post-COVID, and they didn't need this messiness on their hands.

On the call, I explained that they had a responsibility to make their crew feel seen and cared for. I reminded them that, with crew coming from more than 60 countries, this ship was literally the only place some of them could feel pride. "Listen, I don't need a Pride party," I said. "I am a white man from America. But call me Katniss Everdeen and let me volunteer as tribute, because these people need someone to use their privilege and stand up for them. Apparently, you won't, so I will."

Much to my surprise, once again, everyone seemed to be on my side. The president of the company said he found it unacceptable that any higher up onboard the ship would say something that went so directly against the company's ethos. The head of HR promised that not only would we, in fact, be having a Pride party, but that there would be a Pride party on every ship with crew onboard.

It was a win! Standing my ground and using my voice had made a difference. I took down the video and got to tell everyone onboard that we had a party to plan. And a party we had! There was entertainment, food, drinks, and the majority of the ship had a great time. I'm sure there were a few men who stayed in their cabins scratching their heads (compliments of the three-in-one shampoo, conditioner, and body wash they used), but, oh well! Fuck those guys.

With the party behind us, I assumed this chapter was over, but the day after the festivities, I got another text message from Bea asking me to call her when I had a moment. When I gave her a ring on my next break, I expected her to ask if we had been taken care of or how the general vibe on the ship was now that corporate had given them an earful about inclusion. But that's not what happened. Instead, I got an ass-chewing (not in a good way). Bea yelled about how I had broken the ship's social media policy and jeopardized her reputation. Then she *demanded* that I not post on social media for the remainder of the contract.

Well, thank you, Bea, because this fracture in our working relationship catapulted me into taking a chance on myself. For years now, I had been Bea's star singer. I got all the best contracts, and she constantly praised me and my work and was more than happy to take credit for "finding me" when the ship's higher-ups and our guests were happy with my performance. And now here she was chastising me for risking *her* reputation rather than supporting me in fighting for my and my co-workers' rights to be recognized as equally valuable to the company and the ship as the other men onboard, those "men" who didn't want to give my community *one* night to have a party celebrating our existence. She demanded that I give up my new purpose, not to mention a source of supplemental income. In short, she wanted to control me.

It should come as no shock to you that I told Bea to kiss my ass. Instead of complying with her wishes, I did the exact opposite. From that point forward, I spent every spare minute on the ship investing in and growing my social media platform. I posted every single day.

As the months wore on, Bea made it clear that I was no longer in her good graces. She ignored my requests for assistance with work-related problems. She even offered every member of the cast except me a future contract together. Which was fine, because I had already decided that I was going to take a chance on myself and try to do social media full time when I got home.

The first night I spent back in my apartment after the contract ended, I received an email with the contract offer the rest of my cast had received two months earlier. I replied to that offer with the following:

Hello Bea,

I have to tell you that I am surprised to get your email based on the strain in our relationship the past few months. If I am being honest, I have felt entirely disheartened by how you cast me aside the way you did. For years, I have given you my all. All of my talent, all of my respect, and a big chunk of my life. But the moment you felt like I wasn't beneficial to you, you turned on me. I am writing to let you know that I do not now, or ever again in the future, plan to work with you.

Good luck,

Misha

Bestie, to this day, I have never heard from Bea again.

As you know by now, I *did* take that chance on myself, going against every comfort I had ever known and becoming a full-time creator. And what a life-changing experience it has been! My stories currently have over one billion views. I have more than six million followers on social media. I've also gone on to host one of the most popular comedy podcasts, *The Big Flop*. I have pushed myself to get to this place and learned along the way that I can do anything I put my mind to.

I have a lot of friends who still work for Bea. Every so often, one of them tells me that someone will say something like, "Oh my gosh, have you seen what Misha's up to? Isn't that cool?" And every time, Bea sneers in response and says that I am dead to her. As I've been writing about how I have continued to grow my brand, make strides in my business, and help people feel better about themselves *despite* Bea, it's given me an opportunity to reflect on how I have found success completely outside of her guidance, which has only affirmed how much I didn't need it to begin with.

I want you to think about how you can shine in the spotlight you've built. Can you think of a time when you were being shaped or praised by someone? Maybe they were a boss, a mentor, even your parents. And you got their praise as long as you stayed beneficial to them, in their perfectly selfish mold they created.

Here's what I want you to do:

- Reflect on the price you had to pay to stay in their good graces. What pieces of yourself did you have to hide away or change?
- Consider how much you benefited from this relationship compared to how much they benefited. Does the give-and-take with them in your life feel balanced?
- Speak up for yourself even if you think they won't like it. If you're worried about setting a boundary, how much trust do you actually have with them?

- This is the most important part: Write a letter to yourself. No matter where you are currently with living as someone else's mold of you, I want you to write to the version of yourself that finally spoke up or walked away. And I want you to say to yourself, "I'm proud of you." Remember that they didn't reject you. You rejected their ability to control you.

So, Bestie, the next time someone turns on you, rejects you in any way, or reveals their true motives for keeping you around, I want you to dig deep, handle the situation with grace, and understand there's more for you out there. You should *never, ever* have to beg someone to see you. Instead, let it be motivation to work harder and learn more. Take it from me: Although they sting in the moment, situations like this can be the catalyst that propels you to make new choices and discover how capable and powerful you really are. These are the moments that can set you free.

You should never, ever have to beg someone to see you.

CHAPTER 12

I'D RATHER DIE ALONE THAN PUT UP WITH YOUR SHIT

Hey, Bestie! Who doesn't love a good old-fashioned scary story? Let's take a moment right now to sit around the campfire, where I'll share some of the horror stories that have haunted me over the years. These stories have to do with the scariest topic of all: trying to run away from a shitty relationship the same way a busty blonde runs for her life in a slasher film. Like, girl, you are tripping and falling all over yourself, and *stop looking back*, he's not going to change.

Luckily, these tales end like any good scary story does: with the villain being laid to rest. As a bonus, the protagonists all ultimately decided they'd rather take their chances in the haunted woods than spend one more second with the *real* monster. And doesn't spending some time alone sound way better than being metaphorically axe-murdered on a daily basis?

Before I put the proverbial flashlight under my chin, I want to be clear about one thing: There is no such thing as a perfect relationship—and even good ones go through ups and downs, highs and lows. These stories aren't about that. These stories are about our fellow Besties discovering what their hard outs are—and then acting on them. Even when it feels scary.

Once upon a time, I made a video about how easy it is to hold on to the *idea* of a relationship or cling to one or two good things about a person, ignoring the obvious red flags in the process. A few days after posting that video, I got a message from one of my followers telling me that she had started to cry as she watched it. She explained that reality crashed into her like a wave, and all at once, it became clear to her that she had spent the last *12 years* feeling unhappy in her marriage, holding on to the man her husband had promised to be, rather than acknowledging the man he actually was.

She knew she had to leave—and she did. Of course, nobody likes to be rejected, but her soon-to-be ex *really* didn't handle it very well. This is how she said their last conversation went.

> **Douchebag:** *I hope you know how dumb you are. You are a fat 40-year-old single mother of three. Nobody is going to want your used-up body, so good luck being alone for the rest of your life.*
>
> **Bestie:** *Greg, I'm going to give you a reality check, which is, funnily enough, the only check you've received in a while. I didn't leave you for someone else, I left you because you aren't good enough for me. I am done letting a man who looks like a condom filled with cottage cheese tell me when I've had enough to eat. I am done staying with you because you are the human equivalent of Behind on Child Support. I just need to believe I can handle shit on my own. I am done with you being a little boy who mocks my body because I was blessed to be a mother. I am sure you will have terrible things to say about me, but when you have those thoughts, please remember that I think you are the boy that peaked in high school even though you scream at the TV during football games about people's athleticism and criticize their performance from your recliner. You get winded from taking out the trash and can barely get through nine holes of golf with a cart. Not to mention, I've had to be on top for the last three years*

because of your knee. You may wish me ill will, but I won't return that same sentiment. I am finally focused on me.

First of all, she devoured him! The knee comment had me in stitches for days. My girl really said, *Oh! You want to go low? I'll see you in hell!* And also, I was so proud of this Bestie for standing up for herself. To think how she must have felt all those years when her partner was shaming her body because it had changed after having children. Which *he* participated in, by the way.

What really stood out to me, though, is that she didn't leave this loser by replacing him with someone else. She left to fall back in love with herself. That takes a lot of guts, and I hope she got there. (Bestie, DM me with an update if you read this!) I also hope she's gotten herself into a few more positions, if you know what I mean.

Next up is a story about a breakup my friend Sarah went through. One morning I woke up to a message from her, telling me that the guy she had been seeing for seven months had broken up with her via text. She sent me a screenshot because she knows I'm the king of petty comebacks and she wanted my help forming a response. Here's what we were working with:

Um so this is gonna be awkward but Ive been thinking a lot about us and honestly I'm done. Im just speaking my truth but your "independence" is messing with with what we could have been. Like ive told you that it would mean a lot to me if you let me order for you when we go out because it's in my dna to TAKE CARE OF YOU, you immaculate me. I get that your picky but its like you don't trust me that I know you. And Im sorry to bring this up again but I'm just not over you choosing to go to Briannas wedding when you KNEW I wanted to take you to have dinner with my brother when he was in town and go see Inside Out 2. you don't seem to care that I'm the only one making sacrifices here and a real relationship is about compromise from BOTH of us. So yeah I'm out. Good luck with your career and your precious friends and your solo meals.

Yes, you read that grammatical mess right. This man broke up with his girlfriend because he was sad he didn't get to see *Inside Out 2*. LOL!

I suggested that Sarah respond to this block of text with a single line: *I think you mean *emasculate**.

Now, I know you might be wondering why I'm telling you a story about a friend being broken up with when this chapter is about choosing to be by yourself. Well, Bestie, read on.

Inside Out 2 Guy continued to text Sarah over the next few days, going on about all of the ways she hadn't lived up to his expectations of what a woman should be. Sarah shared these messages with me over lunch a few days later and again asked for my opinion about how to reply.

"Don't," I told her as grease from my double bacon cheeseburger dribbled down my wrists.

"I don't know," Sarah replied uncertainly. "I just feel like I owe him a response. We were together for long enough that he deserves to know how I feel."

"*He* ended things," I reminded her. "And he's been talking to you like garbage. Just because he used to have access to your time and feelings doesn't mean he still needs it. Why does he get to act like he's calling the customer service line of your relationship, where he gets to dump all his feelings on you and then it's your job to explain how things actually work to him? Let him go."

Sarah still seemed unsure, so I encouraged her to consider how continuing to engage with her ex would benefit her. She couldn't think of an answer. I then asked her how it would benefit her if she *didn't* respond.

"Well," Sarah said thoughtfully, "I could move on." She paused for a moment. "I could keep my dignity and not give away any of my power."

We love to hear it.

As Sarah discovered, there is never a need for you to chase someone who has shown you their ass. If you are responding or otherwise continuing to engage with someone just to prove that you are right, worthy, or important . . . just don't. All you're actually doing is wasting time and energy on someone who doesn't deserve it. For as much as I love a good comeback, sometimes silence is a way worse burn than anything even I could tell you to say.

Having said all of that, I don't want to ignore the fact that ending a relationship can be hard—because it can. My best friend Courtney—the same girl who you might remember made me mocktails on my first sober New Year's Eve—is one of the strongest people I know. We have been each other's number one ever since we met during our first year of college, way back in 2005, no matter how much physical distance has come between us over the decades.

After I moved away to New York City to pursue my dreams, Courtney met a boy named Donny. Donny quickly filled my role as Courtney's everyday man; they were inseparable. The two of them used to gross me out during the first couple of years of their relationship because they quite literally couldn't keep their hands off each other. But grossness aside, I was so happy that Courtney had found her person.

Years went by, and Courtney and Donny became practically synonymous. They worked together, lived together, did everything together. Eventually, they got married. They went through it all together: money troubles, losing pets, moving, and anything and everything else life had to throw at them. Until Donny lost Courtney's trust, that is.

One night while I happened to be visiting, Courtney discovered inappropriate text messages between Donny and a girl they both worked with. The discovery of those messages marked the beginning of a dark time in my best friend's life. Courtney is *the* most loyal person I know; she loves with her entire being. So to have the blind faith she'd had in the person who was her entire universe disintegrate was debilitating.

But despite her never trusting Donny again, they stayed together. The fear of losing him, of being alone, won every battle Courtney waged in her head. It was sad to watch as they lost the sparkle they'd once had—gross or not.

Flash-forward a couple of years: Courtney was getting ready to start a new career just as her mom received a very serious cancer diagnosis. Donny became resentful of Courtney's frequent absence as she balanced trying to better herself and her future, while also caring for her mother. He ended up being unfaithful again—and leaving Courtney this time.

Courtney's other friends and I did our best to assure her she was better off without a guy who would betray her like this and worth so much more than what she was getting, but still, she was devastated.

Donny came back about six months later. Courtney did her best to prove to him that she was worth choosing. But how do you come back from the infidelity, abandonment, and disregard? Their relationship lasted a couple more very difficult years before finally coming to an end once and for all. In that time, Courtney became a shell of the girl I had known. I can't remember a phone call we had during that time that didn't end with her in tears.

Eventually, Courtney slowly started picking up the pieces of her shattered heart. Her mom went into remission, Courtney got a new job, and, as she liked to say, she "kept it moving."

Courtney embodied what it means to not give up. For as much pain as she was in, she was also full of hope and understood she had an opportunity to find out just how strong she was. I cheered her on as she learned how to care for herself in a more complete way than she had when she was wasting all of that energy and attention on someone else.

Not too long ago, Courtney met someone new and they started dating. Courtney pushed through her initial hesitation to open up to someone again and let herself be excited about a budding new romance. Unfortunately, her mom became sick again around the same time because life fucking sucks sometimes. Courtney resumed the role of taking care of her mom.

One evening, Courtney was hanging out with her new boyfriend when it became clear he was trying to hide something on his phone. She asked to see it, and he admitted that he'd recently downloaded a dating app. He tried to defend himself, saying that he had *only* downloaded it, he'd only done so recently, and it was only because Courtney was so emotionally absent due to working full time and taking care of her mom. He felt lonely, he explained. (Cue the tiniest violin.)

This time around, Courtney wasn't having it. She knew she deserved more and that this was a dealbreaker. Calmly, she explained that she'd been through this before, and this time, she was choosing herself.

I hope Courtney knows how proud I am of her and that I see how much she's grown and how strong she is. Witnessing her evolution has inspired me more than she will probably ever understand.

And I know you're strong too, Bestie. Here's the thing though: Many people make a list of what they *want* in a partner, but fewer sit down and define what they *don't* want. Your standards aren't too high, he's just short.

I want you to get out your journal and start a list of "Things I Will Not Put Up With." This is not a wish list, Bestie, it's a self-respect contract.

When you have your hell-no list, I want you to consider the following questions:

- When was the last time I ignored my gut or something on this list and gave someone a second, third, hell, even a fourth chance that they didn't earn? What did it cost me?

- Am I willing to make this list my hard outs? No matter how charming or sexy they are?
- If someone crosses one of these boundaries I've written in permanent marker, how do I want to handle it? Get clarity? Silence? Slam the door in their damn face? It's your choice, Bestie.
- What message will I be sending to myself if I don't enforce my boundaries? And what do I want to be sending instead?

Listen, romance doesn't have to be perfect. Believe it or not, there *are* relationships that are worth fighting for—but those relationships won't require you to lose pieces of yourself along the way. If you find that happening, know that while the thought of being alone can feel scarier than staying in an unsatisfying or unhealthy relationship, it's just a mirage. If you dig deep, I bet you'll realize that what *actually* feels scary is having to face the uncomfortable feelings that come along with all of this, as well as the uncertainty.

But I promise you this: There is so much beauty in dealing with those feelings. Choose to love yourself first.

“Just because he used to have access to your time and feelings doesn't mean he still needs it.”

CHAPTER 13

YOU CAN BE THE JUICIEST PEACH—BUT NOT EVERYONE LIKES PEACHES

Hey, Bestie! I want to start this chapter by saying I'm *so* damn proud of you. You have been working hard and digging deep to figure out who you are and who you want to be, and believing wholeheartedly that you are enough. Now it's time to take all that work and start *being* it—unapologetically.

You want to be liked, respected, loved, and adored. I get it. But what you shouldn't do is mold and bend yourself to fit into someone else's approval puzzle. Your job is to be you, and if that doesn't work for other people, that's a problem for them, not you.

The online landscape is full of contrarians, people who love to feel morally superior, and people who still read at a fifth-grade level (I can spot these people immediately because they never seem to know the difference between *your* and *you're*—see Chapter 12 for reference). Even though I put myself out there on social media knowing that I would absolutely receive criticism, when I first started posting, the people-pleaser in me still used to spiral a little bit when negativity or disapproval was directed my way. Sometimes it felt like people wanted to hold me accountable for what I had to say more than they wanted to hold a bully accountable who chose to tear somebody else down for their actions.

It didn't bother me so much when I was criticized by the obviously homophobic dipshits who would hate me even if I cured their limp dick, but it definitely got to me when that criticism came from people who just didn't seem to like me. In those moments, my internal dialogue went something like this: *I'm just trying to be nice and funny. Why don't you see that?* Even worse were the people who followed me, seemed to like me, and then decided they were no longer interested in being one of my besties.

I let these comments get to me, and for a while, I was so concerned with how I would be perceived that I edited my videos down to a bland version of myself, like a once-crisp iced tea that had been left sitting out in the sun for too long.

But I soon found that the more I catered my content to try to please everyone, the worse it performed. I learned that, for me at least, if what I had to say didn't challenge people, then it probably wasn't worth sharing in the first place. I stopped qualifying everything I had to say in an effort to minimize potential blowback from people who didn't want to like my content in the first place. Instead, I started aggressively being myself.

I had to let the "not all men," "not all straight people," and "not all Boomers" comments roll off my back. I slowly realized that I never felt bad about what I was creating as long as I stayed true to myself. I even decided it was actually a blessing for the handful of people who did walk away to do so. I also learned when to stand up for myself and when to shrug my shoulders and understand that I just wasn't for some people, and that engaging wasn't worth my energy.

With a little practice, it's easy enough to dismiss people who you don't respect, who don't deserve your kindness, or who don't live a life that resembles the one you want to live. But what about the people you *do* respect or emulate? How can you navigate tension with (or even rejection from) them?

Story incoming: One afternoon a notification popped up on my phone, letting me know that an actor and trailblazer in the LGBTQ community had started following me. For anonymity's sake, let's call her Cassie. Not only did Cassie follow me, but she also used the audio from one of my videos to lip sync and make her own video. It was new and exciting for me to receive this kind of acknowledgment from a celebrity—especially one I looked up to.

Just a few weeks later this icon sent me a message on social media. I got butterflies when her name popped up because what could Cassie possibly want to chat about with me? Well, let's just say that excitement wore off rather quickly when I read what she had written:

> *Misha. Please excuse the unwelcome sneak into your DMs. I don't do this a lot honestly, and I want to start off by saying I think you're hilarious!! I also think you're smart and very savvy. And . . . I think you're much kinder than your videos lead others to believe. I've watched many of your vids and I love them for what they're TRYING to do. But I feel the approach may be sending a message you're not aware of. I wholeheartedly agree with [your message], but I think you might have forgotten it somewhere along the way. Look, I love a good Joan Rivers dig as much as the next human, but Joan made jokes because she was a teacher. She was teaching us the idiocy of complacency and prejudice.*

Cassie went on to say that she also believed my videos weren't reaching the people who needed to learn the lessons the most. That my sharp tongue would turn off all the bigots and incels of the world, and how could they ever learn to be kind to people like me if they couldn't hear me?

She was advocating for the old you-catch-more-flies-with-honey-than-vinegar tactic. But all I took away from her message was that this hero of mine, this person who I had (and still have) a lot of respect for and who has contributed so much to the world—thought my videos were dumbed down and unkind. I felt embarrassed and, also, a little resentful. Her words felt like an accusation against me, rather than an open dialogue to try to understand me.

Believe me, I had received my fair share of "feedback" that I was mean before Cassie reached out. But my stance has remained the same: I. Don't. Care. I will never understand why people are more concerned about the feelings of the bully than the feelings of the person being bullied. Make it make sense. I am here to uplift those people who have been targeted by bullies, *not* to plummet my own IQ by trying to teach some dum-dum to be nice. This is more than just clapping back, like we've talked about already. This is about understanding for yourself that not everyone will like you or understand you, and you knowing that that's okay.

When I responded to Cassie's message, I tried to explain *my* page through *my* lens. I wrote from my heart and approached her criticism with respect. I told her how much I appreciated her, and that I had truly absorbed what she had written to me. But I also stood my ground and said that I believed what I was doing was true to me. I explained that I am always concerned with my personal growth, that I consider the world around me and how I affect it, and I do my best to make sure that my actions match my words. I also pushed back a little and told her I didn't agree that my videos weren't reaching the right people. My videos have always been *for* the people who feel beaten down. I'm not trying to teach the bullies—I'm trying to nurture those who are being bullied.

Finally, I shared that I had received thousands of messages from all sorts of humans, telling me how my words had helped them through dark times, inspired them to step into their power, and even made them realize that gay people aren't bad. In other words, I was getting direct feedback that contradicted her opinion.

I walked away from my messages feeling like I had done myself justice. I was polite in my response and stayed true to who I was. I was sure this was going to start an open dialogue and potentially mark the beginning of a new friendship.

Well, Cassie clearly didn't see things from my point of view because she blocked me after reading my message. At first, I started reeling through that familiar spiral of self-doubt. I wanted to scream: I'M JUST TRYING TO BE NICE AND FUNNY. WHY DON'T YOU SEE THAT? For days, I had that feeling you get in the pit of your stomach when you've done something bad and are waiting to get caught—except I also didn't feel like I had done anything wrong.

I think that it's crucial to be open to criticism, and to be willing to listen and learn from others—*especially* from people you respect. No matter how much work we do or how self-aware we are, there's always room to grow. But there will also be moments when you'll have to take in constructive feedback from people you respect, admire, or are close to, and then decide whether or not it feels appropriate to adjust accordingly. Sometimes the answer will be yes. And other times you will choose to stand your ground, knowing this means you are also making the choice to dissent from that person—or even have them walk away from you. I won't lie, this is extremely uncomfortable at first if you are like me and have been known to be a people pleaser in a past life!

When I got honest with myself, it became clear that even though I believed I was right to stand my ground, the fact that someone who I would love to be friends with thought badly of me was driving me nuts. Plain and simple.

And then I thought about my nana.

When I was very young—maybe nine years old—I threw the front door open one day after school and went flying directly into my mom's arms, sobbing uncontrollably because the kids at school had called me a faggot and a flamer. It was all because of Celine Dion's iconic song, "My Heart Will Go On." I was obsessed and wanted to perform it with a group of my friends at school. We spent days practicing for the big performance in the music room during our lunch period. The plan was that I would sing the first verse as a solo, and then everyone else would chime in and we'd perform the rest as a group. Our teacher had arranged for us to give our one-night-(er, day)-only, star-studded performance during lunch, because the lunchroom conveniently had a stage.

Maybe you can already guess what happened, Bestie. Well, maybe you can't because I actually started the song by playing the flute intro. Yes! I play the flute. No wonder they all thought I was a flamer, LOL.

Imagine a bunch of rambunctious kids eating their lunch when, all of a sudden, this familiar angelic tune rings through the cafetorium. They look up to see my bleached blonde self and a handful of my friends standing onstage creating these dulcet sounds. After the flute cameo, I started singing and the roaring laughter commenced almost immediately—but I pushed through the rest of that damn song because we worked so hard to learn it.

I was picked on relentlessly for the rest of the day. Those stupid little lunchtime twerps stripped me of any feeling of pride I deserved for my Grammy-worthy performance and instead left me feeling ashamed for liking anything outside the "normal" boy-approved things.

Did I mention this happened during my first year at this school? My dad had just left the military, and I was trying to find my place in a new town. In fact, my family was so freshly moved that we were still living with my nana and papa while my parents searched for a house. This was okay with me, because my grandparents were my favorite people.

Things were good at home—but things felt hard at school as I tried to carve out a place to fit in. And this incident made me feel like I never would, no matter how hard I tried.

As soon as I left that stage, all I could think about was getting out of that school and back to my mom. Once I collapsed in her arms, I let myself fall apart—that kind of crying where you can't catch a breath. Where it hurts like how I imagine drowning would be—but in a sea of being called a "faggot" and not being able to breathe. I couldn't get any words out, but in my head I was screaming, *WHY DON'T THEY LIKE ME?*

The day after my meltdown, Nana invited me to help her make her famous peanut butter cookies. I happily agreed because I just so happened to be Nana's favorite person and I knew I would get to lick the cookie dough off the beater. (I don't want to hear about the raw egg, Bestie—I survived!)

My nana was the total cliché of a grandma, and I could do absolutely no wrong in her eyes. There was one time that all the theatre kids (me included) got suspended for getting stoned at Gabby's house before rehearsal when I was in high school. Well, as soon as Nana found out about this, she marched her ass over to the school and right into the principal's office. "How dare you suspend my grandson?" she demanded.

I was mortified when I found out about this because, of course, I *had* gotten stoned. When I told Nana as much, she shrugged her shoulders and said, "I don't care if you did it! You're special!" So you see? Whether I was getting high before rehearsal or wine drunk at family gatherings, her love for me never wavered.

As we were making the cookies and I was making a mess, Nana asked if I wanted to talk about what had happened at school. I felt embarrassed as I told her what the kids had called me and hung my head as I said, "I'm sorry."

Nana put down that electric hand mixer and looked me straight in the eyes. "You don't have to apologize for those assholes," she said, enunciating each word loudly and clearly. (See where I get it, Bestie?)

As I licked that delicious *E. coli*–free batter, the two of us had a long chat about how I was feeling at my new school. "I just want my classmates to like me, but I feel like nothing I do works," I confided.

And that's when Nana told me something that still echoes in my head to this day. "That's because you are meant to stand out," Nana said. "You can be the nicest, funniest, smartest person around, and there will still always be people who just don't like you. But it's your job to be yourself, whether they like it or not."

If I'm being honest, it still stings when someone who I like and want to be friends with doesn't feel the same. But I've finally gotten to the place where, despite the sting of it, I can understand that we just don't agree, and that's okay. I don't have to apologize or change or hide who I am and what I believe in because of it.

Both my experiences with Cassie and a bunch of kids who I haven't seen in decades gave me the chance to pause, reflect, and realize that I didn't need external validation—even from people I respect. Finally, I had arrived at a place where I could validate myself. How freaking cool is that?

I'm not going to allow anyone else to control my language, explain what my messaging should be, or in any other way place their expectations upon me. I can stand firm in my belief that I am doing something good—and it's okay if not everyone understands.

So, Bestie, it is up to you to choose those moments in your life when it feels appropriate to be open to others' opinions and maybe even absorb some of their beliefs into your life. It's equally important to understand when to stand your ground and remain strong and consistent in what you do and believe—even in the face of people who you admire and respect, people who you like and who you want to like you.

Here's your task at hand:

1. Think of a piece of criticism that has stuck with you. Who gave it? Did this person have your best interest at heart?

2. Ask yourself, is this about me or them? Does their feedback help me grow in any way? Does it align with what I know to be true for me?

3. Trust your gut. Don't react out of fear or ego.

4. Really think about how you receive feedback. It's important to recognize when the feedback challenges you and helps you see blind spots in your life. We want people who love us enough to be honest . . . and kind. But there are also judgment and projection to consider. Is this person trying to control you or turn you into something they approve of? Go back to your gut.

How does their opinion make you feel? Can you see where they are coming from? Does their opinion feel like an attack? Can you envision a future version of yourself as the person they have encouraged you to become? And, if so, does that feel like a version of you that *you'll* love? Or are they trying to control and change you into a version of yourself that doesn't feel right?

There are literally billions of people in the world, so if one person wants to walk away from the shiny, amazing, beautiful, funny, fuzzy little peach that you are . . . let them. Even when it feels hard or disappointing. Because at the end of the day, the only person who really needs to choose you is *you*.

Your job is to be you, and if that doesn't work for other people, that's a problem for them, not you.

CHAPTER 14

I'M NOT BOSSY, I'M THE BOSS

Hey, Bestie! Now that you're getting used to standing your ground with other people, it's time you start standing your ground with *yourself* as well. And by that I mean: Stop second-guessing your gut when it's trying to lead you in the right direction. Stop wondering if you are really ready. You are. You've done the work and it's time to stand up to yourself and not shrink back into old habits.

I know that I have gone against my better judgment in the past for any number of reasons: trying to be a team player, putting other people's feelings ahead of my own, and being too afraid to take a risk, just to name a few. But now that I'm a lot more comfortable with who I am and what I want, I'm so much better at paying attention to that nagging feeling in my stomach whenever she just can't seem to keep it to herself.

When I was pursuing theatre, my lack of trust in myself came up a lot. Kind of like the military, the world of theatre has a hierarchy that is never really questioned. Seriously, why do you think there are a bunch of older men from the entertainment industry who are rotting in prison (which is exactly where they belong) for abusing their positions of power and weaponizing them against others?

That's an extreme example, but I worked at theatres with people who made racist remarks, sexually harassed those "below" their rank, and were even abusive in certain instances. And while there were a handful of times I caused a scene about it like the tornado that I can be, most of the time I suppressed my feelings about those injustices and stayed in my lane. Not because I didn't care, but because we all thought that's just how things were.

The world is full of people who will try to take advantage of you. It was true in my previous career, and it's certainly true in my current career as an Internet celebrity, that some people may see you only as potential dollar signs for them. I learned this lesson in the course of a truly bizarre few months with my first-ever social media manager, who we'll call Suzie.

About four months into being a full-time content creator, I reached the one million followers milestone. This was a shit-my-pants moment for me, but it didn't mean that I wasn't still broke; I definitely was. Right around that time, a woman who I had become online friends with asked if she could introduce me to a manager she knew named Suzie.

The world of social media was still relatively new to me, but like most of us, I had heard how much money influencers could make, so I was freaking out on the inside. It was an immediate *yes* from me, Bestie! We scheduled that meeting faster than most men take to disappoint you. I was so excited for my life to change.

The very same day that I was scheduled to meet with Suzie I just so happened to receive an email offering me my first-ever brand deal. It was from an eyewear company, and they were offering me $2,000 to make one video. I honestly couldn't believe it, and I was excited to be able to share news of this development with Suzie on our call later that day.

When we hopped onto our virtual meeting, I was thrilled to see that Suzie was *exactly* what I had envisioned—the cliché Los Angeles talent manager, dressed in all black, including the oversize black-frame glasses that took up way too much space on her very angular face. Every word she said was spoken with the heaviest vocal fry I had ever heard. She reminded me of a Disney villain like Cruella de Vil or Yzma—but a villain who was promising to make me The Next Big Thing. I, like most of the world, just assumed that this was how all LA talent managers were, so she was *exactly* who I thought I needed to be talking to.

Suzie told me about a client she represented who had become well known on home renovation shows in the early 2000s. Like most of America, I had seen those shows, so I was impressed. However, I also noticed that this was the *only* celebrity Suzie mentioned representing. Maybe she just didn't want to brag? Suzie went on to explain that getting into the digital space and working with influencers was a new venture for her. She described working with a few other people I wasn't familiar with, but she folded that piece of information in quickly amid pitching her work ethic and bullish nature.

In all fairness, I did wonder, *So . . . am I a guinea pig?* But my excitement overshadowed my gut recognition that Suzie didn't seem to have a ton of experience working with people in my field.

After listening to Suzie pitch herself (and feeling nervous the entire time that the strain of the vocal fry might actually rupture her vocal cords), it was my turn to try to impress her. At this point in my brand-new career, I thought *my* pitch was the most important part of the meeting and that *I* needed to impress *her*. This was easy enough because I did bring to the table a referral, a lot of followers, and that deal with the eyewear company. In addition, I also happen to be very charming. I talked about my theatre background and all the talents I could tap into, my own work ethic, and how I was ready to go after this 100 percent. Oh, and I also let her know that I am fun to work with. Basically, Bestie, I slayed.

I *must* have slayed, because Suzie told me that she would love to represent me before we even got off the call. She said she was ready to take over negotiations for the eyewear brand deal and get to work creating even more opportunities for my impending stardom. It sounded great, but once again my gut piped in, this time alerting me that we might be moving a little too fast. After all, Suzie and I hadn't even discussed important logistics, like if we were going to sign a contract, how much commission she was going to take, or, probably most bizarrely, what her damn email address was. That's right: I literally didn't even know how to get ahold of my new manager.

Nevertheless, after reaching out to my friend who had introduced us to ask for Suzie's email and phone number, I agreed to work with her. And we did not, in fact, sign a contract of any kind.

Our first order of business was finalizing the already-existing brand deal. I forwarded Suzie the email I had received from the eyewear company and let her take over. For the next couple of days, Suzie negotiated the partnership while I daydreamed about all the possibilities that lay before me. I was stuffing a baja shrimp taco into my face when my phone lit up with an email notification from Suzie, saying that she had convinced the eyewear brand to bring the offer up from $2,000 to $3,000—for one social media video! Maybe all of my reservations were for naught.

I was extremely grateful for this opportunity. I had worked hard on my social media and really needed that money. And I also knew how wild it was to get paid to post on social media, so I was absolutely thrilled. Sure, it wasn't the life-changing money that some influencers claim they make for brand deals, but it was a perfect way to start the next phase of my career *and* my new relationship with Suzie.

The eyewear brand partnership went smoothly. The content I made performed well on social media, and a month later I got paid and promptly sent Suzie her 20 percent cut. I was more than content with our arrangement and happy I hadn't had to spend any time going back and forth with the eyewear company to make it all happen.

After that, things with Suzie started to get weird. I didn't hear from her for long stretches of time. When I reached out to ask for updates, if anything was in the works, or if I could do anything on my end, she responded by telling me things like, "I actually have a meeting with FOX this afternoon to pitch you for some show ideas," or "I'm compiling a list of brands I think we need to target, and maybe change your content a bit—I think it's just too ahead of its time." Or my fav, "I had lunch with a producer yesterday who is *dying* to work with you. Can't tell you who it is yet, babe—NDA vibes—but it's major!" Of course, Suzie was just blowing smoke up my you-know-what and none of those things actually panned out.

This went on for a few months. The only actual movement we had was another offer from that same eyewear company. They said they had enjoyed working with me and offered a long-term partnership. The good news was they wanted to work together for eight months! The bad news was they wanted to bring the price back down to their original offer of $2,000 per post. Suzie went back and forth with them but ultimately didn't get them to budge on their price. I appreciated the opportunity and accepted it, but all my red flags about Suzie were blowing at full mast by this point.

I was growing increasingly aware that Suzie was collecting 20 percent of a deal I had gotten on my own, while contributing nothing in the five months we had "worked" together. I wouldn't hear from Cruella—sorry! I mean *Suzie*—for weeks at a time, but you better believe she texted me within minutes of my payout from the eyewear company reminding me to pay her share.

That summer, another opportunity that had nothing to do with Suzie came to me in the form of some good PR. *USA Today* reached out because they wanted to include me in an article they were writing about TikTok influencers who were changing the comedy scene. Bestie, this was a huge moment for me. Not only was I being recognized in a major publication, but some of my very favorite comedians and creators were also included in the article. It was one of those pinch-me moments.

Upon publication, the article immediately drew attention my way. In addition to getting new followers, I also received emails from PR agencies who wanted to work with me, as well as interview requests from other publications. Oh, and I also started to get emails from other management companies that wanted to represent me.

My first instinct was to turn them down because I was already "signed" with Suzie and couldn't under any circumstances fuck her over. That's just not how I'm built. Each time I deleted an email, I tried to ignore that persistent gut feeling that I was making the wrong decision. I honestly think my resistance was because I didn't want to face the truth that I had jumped the gun and signed with someone I didn't investigate more beforehand.

Even so, I eventually *did* take a meeting with one of the PR agencies because the person who emailed mentioned that she was a longtime follower of mine and I will always give a bestie my time. During the meeting, we talked about a lot of different aspects of the creator space, and I decided to ask her opinion about my Suzie predicament. She told me that I was, indeed, being played and, not only that, but I was also losing out on opportunities by refusing meetings with potentially legitimate management companies. Even though I didn't end up working with this particular PR company, this woman was a true bestie, and she gave me an email contact at an agency she knew to be highly respected.

I promise this next part of the story is true: I emailed the address my new PR bestie had just given me, explaining who I was and that I had been referred to them. I hit the send button and immediately received an email from that very same management company. The email came so immediately that I initially thought I had been given a bogus email address and was receiving one of those bounce-back return-to-sender emails in response. But I looked more closely and sure enough! It was an actual email from some guy named Phil.

The email didn't make sense to me at first because Phil was telling *me* who *he* was. As I read, I thought, *Yes, okay, ho. I literally just emailed you; obviously I know who you are.* But, Bestie, it turns out that Phil and I had emailed each other *at the same exact time.* Some clients of his were included in the same *USA Today* article, and it put me on his radar. We just so happened to have arrived at the same point at the very same moment.

I was *really* excited because this wasn't just a person, it was a whole-ass agency. An agency with clients I very much recognized! The day of the meeting with Phil, I hyped myself up before the call and reminded myself to ask the questions I knew I needed answers to. My less-than-stellar experience with Suzie had taught me that. But all that hyping up and reminding turned out to be unnecessary because the meeting with Phil and his colleague, Chris, was a totally different experience from my initial meeting with Suzie. Phil and Chris showed up ready to fully communicate what they did, what they offered, what they expected, and how things worked. In the end, I didn't have to ask all the questions I had prepared because they answered them of their own accord.

Most notably, they were offering a *contract.* (Bestie, if there is one thing you take away from this, let it be the importance of a contract!) Before I signed, I told them about my Suzie situation and that I couldn't agree to anything before speaking with her. But my mind was already made up.

I sent an email to Suzie letting her know that the time had come for us to part ways because I was getting ready to sign with a bigger agency. I was polite and didn't feel the need to turn our parting into a big dramatic affair when it didn't need to be. Suzie responded that she understood. I was still in the middle of my long-term contract with the eyewear brand, and Suzie *had* been a part of it, so we agreed that I would pay out her share of the money through the duration of the contract. This was an easy decision because it seemed only fair. Relieved and excited to move on, I figured that was the end of that.

I signed my new contract, feeling good about both my decision and the amicable parting of ways Suzie and I had, so I was shocked when I received an email from Suzie telling me that she had decided she also deserved 20 percent on any *future* contracts I might have with the eyewear company, because, after all, she was the reason I had that business at all.

Um, *excuse me*? Suzie's beatnik-looking ass didn't do anything besides get me that extra grand for the first video. I replied that any future contracts would be renegotiated with my new management team, so our working relationship—and any payments—would be over at the end of the current eyewear contract.

Biiiiiiiiiiiiiitch, why did this ridiculous woman then decide to go *behind my back* and email the eyewear brand directly, saying that she needed to be included in any future offers with me or they would be prohibited from ever working with me again? Apparently, the brand thought this was strange, so they sent me an email directly to ask if everything was okay. I politely informed them that Suzie was, in fact, unhinged. I also told them that I loved working with them and directed them to my new management for any future deals.

For someone who allegedly had 25 years' experience in this industry, you'd think Suzie would have known better than to act like a petulant child. I immediately emailed her, demanding that she explain herself. Suzie responded by telling me that she would reach back out to the brand and see if they would be willing to pay a larger fee so that I could pay out both my new managers *and* her for all future contracts that didn't even exist. I told her that she was not to email anyone else in reference to me.

Her response consisted of just two words: "You're bossy."

I swiftly let this delusional woman know that, yes, I was, in fact, the boss.

She came back with the ol' classic: *You'll never work again!*

My last words to Suzie were, "I should have known from your I-just-got-into-witchcraft outfit and bare white wall background that you weren't in a position to help me. And that's on me. But our time working together is over, and I hope you eventually grow up."

To this day, whenever my gut starts speaking, I remind myself of what I learned from Suzie: to trust my initial instincts over my inner nice guy.

Shortly after signing with Phil and Chris, they landed me a $25,000 deal with a global brand. I don't say that to brag, but to point out that Suzie was clearly not even playing the same game as my new managers. They saw my worth, my potential, and my work ethic, and they have matched it with their own every single day. Those are the people I want on my team, and that's where I want to put my energy.

Over to you, my friend. I have an exercise I want you to try out. I want you to draw up a contract with yourself. Think of it like you're both the CEO and employee of your life and you are creating an agreement with yourself that sets up the vision of your higher self.

Here's what you need to include:

- Your non-negotiables. What are the things that you *must* have to be your boss bitch self? In my contract I wrote down that I won't say yes just to keep the peace, I won't ignore red flags even if they are dressed up as opportunity, and I won't stay small to make others comfortable.

- Your intentions. Think about some of the times in your life when you haven't trusted your gut and ignored your intuition. How did you act? What did it feel like? Next, write out how the boss in you will act now that you are being intentional.
- Your declaration. Lastly, I want you to write at the bottom of the contract: "I am no longer shrinking back into old habits. I'm not bossy. I'm the damn boss."
- Your signature and date. This is a contract after all, a promise to yourself, so let's make it official.

So, Bestie, I want to make a deal with you; in fact, you can consider it a binding contract between us. I want you to promise that you won't ignore that little voice inside your head telling you what you really want or need, just to keep the peace or earn the respect of someone who doesn't even get you. You never need to prove your worth, you just need to trust it. Standing up for yourself isn't just setting up boundaries with others, it's also about setting up boundaries with yourself. When your gut starts yelling at you and you feel the urge to second-guess yourself, don't. Stand tall. You are the boss of your own life. *You* get to call the shots.

“Stop second-guessing your gut when it’s trying to lead you in the right direction.”

CHAPTER 15

DON'T LET THE DOOR HIT YOU ON THE WAY OUT

Hey, Bestie! By now we know that when we finally choose to stand up for ourselves (perhaps for the first time ever!), it feels *really good*. We also now know that growing and expanding and continuing to sculpt our badass self involves exorcising negative people from our life, even if it involves allowing those who we love and admire to walk away from us if they choose.

It can certainly be tempting to look at all your relationships in a black-and-white type of way. I know that when I first started standing up for myself, I fell into the trap of becoming such a hard ass with my standards and what I would or would not accept from others that, honestly, I probably permanently deleted some people from my life who didn't need to be forever banished.

But for as much as I pride myself on the work I have done to heal and take care of myself, it took me time to learn that sometimes you can choose to be soft, relinquish control, and allow a relationship the space to evolve as it will in its own time. And I learned this lesson most from a teenage girl named Bean.

Amber and I are lucky enough to have the type of friendship where it feels like no time at all has passed every time we meet again.

We met during our freshman year of college, and our friendship lived on after she transferred to another school the next year. One time, she invited me to come spend her birthday weekend at her new school. Amber was particularly excited about this reunion because she had started seeing a new guy named Dave and she wanted the two of us to meet.

Dave was, to put it nicely, a total fucking douchebag. He was in a fraternity, spent the majority of his time farting in his hand and then placing that hand over other people's faces, and talking incessantly about his high school baseball fame. I found him to be insufferable and hated that Amber had somehow managed to find the most cliché fuckboy on campus to be with. But, of course, I wasn't dating him, and I know that people can be very different when they are in private and feel safe, so I kept my opinion to myself.

Much to my surprise, Amber and Dave stayed together throughout the rest of their college experience, culminating with Amber getting pregnant their senior year. Not surprisingly, they hadn't planned for this to happen and were scared out of their minds, but they seemed committed to making it work and Dave proposed to Amber.

Even after they got married, I still felt the same about Dave as I had when we first met: that he was basically a baby with armpit hair. He was harmless, but just super, *super* annoying.

Bestie, have you ever not liked one of your friends' partners? Like, your friend is a goddess among mortals yet still chooses a guy who struggles to tie his shoes? But as long as they're happy, right? That's what I kept telling myself as I kept my mouth shut and trusted that my friend was making the right decision for herself.

Any reservations I had about Amber and Dave's relationship were immediately overshadowed when Amber called me one day and asked me if I would be willing to be their daughter's godfather. *Daughter!* They were having a little girl! I don't know if my heart has ever burst with as much love as it did in that moment. There was a tiny little princess growing inside one of my best friends and I was going to get to be a huge part of her life!

When I went to meet my goddaughter at the hospital a couple of weeks after she made her debut, I was awestruck by how small she was. "She looks like a little bean," I whispered to Amber.

Ever since that day, I have called my goddaughter Bean. She was small, but she was a fighter and she continued to grow stronger each day. Thanks to Amber and the many doctors and nurses who took care of her, Bean was ready to go home and fully start her little life a couple of months after she was born.

The first few years of Bean's life were mostly normal. She had a doting mother, lots of toys to play with, and was healthy despite the fact that as a preemie, she was on the smaller side for her age. But Amber and Dave weren't doing so well. Amber took her role as a mom seriously, while Dave remained stuck in his high school days. He continued to drink as if he were still living in the old frat house, he avoided responsibility like it would give him cooties, and he couldn't seem to make a job stick for more than a few months.

Amber's entire universe shifted the moment she had Bean, and she was no longer disillusioned about who Dave really was. She called me all the time to complain about whatever his most recent foolish decision was, like the time he took their tax refund and bought a snowmobile—even though they lived in South Carolina, where it hardly ever snows. But like many women in situations like this, she desperately clung to the hope that he would transform into the man he had promised to be for their daughter's sake.

Hostage to that hope, Amber agreed to move to Florida when Dave got a job offer at a construction company. Yes, they would all be starting over again in a town where they didn't know a single soul, but this was Dave's big shot at landing on his feet.

Well, Dave landed on his feet, but he twisted his ankle and fell down hard on his hairy ass. It turned out that this "construction company" was simply an *idea* that a former co-worker of Dave's had dreamed up—except, unfortunately, it never took flight and Dave was, once again, jobless. But this time, his little family had uprooted their entire lives only for him.

Amber was, rightfully, furious, and the whole fiasco created a huge fracture in their relationship. Dave's drinking continued to get worse, and the next couple of years were generally not great. The more Dave resisted growing up, the more tense things grew. What had been acceptable when he actually *was* an idiotic frat boy, was no longer cute.

One day, Amber came home from work to find Dave drunk following a full day of drinking—while watching Bean, who was only six years old at the time. Amber confronted him, and Dave snapped and proceeded to *punch* Amber as Bean watched on. He immediately fled the house, leaving his girls to pick up the shattered pieces of their hearts.

Amber told all of this to me and another friend in a group chat. Bestie, let me tell you, both me and that friend booked a flight to Florida the next day. As soon as we arrived, we all sat in the living room and did what friends do in a situation like this: We let Amber get it *allllllll* out.

In the middle of our conversation, little Bean walked into the room, crying hysterically. At first, we thought she had hurt herself and frantically checked her for cuts or broken bones. Physically, she was fine. But through her sobs she said, "Mommy, I don't ever want to get married." Amber told Bean that she had many years before she had to make that decision and that boys wouldn't always be icky to her.

"No!" Bean protested. "I don't *ever* want to get married because I don't want to get hurt!"

I saw the look on Amber's face and knew that she was about to lose it, so I quickly scooped up Bean and took her into her bedroom to play with Barbies so she wouldn't have to see her mom in even more pain than she had already witnessed. I knew Amber well enough to understand that she would never be able to forgive Dave. But I also knew that she would never be able to forgive herself if she felt like she had shown her daughter that it's okay for love to hurt. She filed for divorce later that week.

Over the next few years, Bean struggled in her relationship with her dad. She loved him so much and couldn't understand why he wasn't around a lot. It seemed that losing his family hadn't taught him anything. He missed birthdays, canceled on Bean at the last minute more times than I can count, and never had the means to contribute financially. All of this affected Bean deeply.

Years passed and I started to build my social media following as Bean was in middle school. She *loved* hearing the stories about me standing up for myself and thought it was incredible that millions of other people were watching those stories too. Bean would ask her mom to watch my videos and then read the comments left by people. And apparently, she was taking notes.

One day Amber called to tell me that Bean got detention—and it was my fault. That morning some mean girls at school had been picking on Bean. They were passing notes in class, looking at Bean, and laughing. Bean stood up and said, "Awwww, you're passing notes and spreading rumors about me? At least you're finally spreading something other than your legs!"

You wouldn't guess it from her clapback, but something you should know about Bean is that she's painfully shy, and this was *very* out of character for her. And Amber was so proud of her. So proud that when I asked her if I could share it on social media, she agreed.

Bean was an instant hit; the Internet ate up the story of her standing up for herself against these middle school bitches. Amber has very strict social media rules for Bean, but she let her watch these videos, as well as read some of the thousands of comments cheering her on. It was a joy to watch Bean experience a sense of pride I hadn't seen in her before and (I believe) a tipping point in who Bean is destined to become.

But as much as Bean and Amber continued to thrive and share their bravery and heart with the world, Dave wasn't consistently present. But life certainly presents us with some gray areas. There might be people who don't fit in to (or want to be in) your life for the moment, but who you don't want to close the door on forever. Not every relationship has to be severed completely. Handling relationships in this kind of nuanced way requires balance and grace, and it can take some practice. One day Dave texted Amber that he was moving to Tennessee to be with a woman he had met online. Amber told him that it didn't matter to her because he didn't contribute anything anyway but that he needed to ask Bean for her blessing. Dave agreed and made plans to pick up Bean and spend the entire day with her the following Saturday.

Bean was so excited. She hadn't spent a day with her dad in a long time and was looking forward to this much-needed quality time. But Saturday came and went, and her dad never showed up—or even called, for that matter. Bean was devastated. Not wanting to lie to her, Amber told Bean that her dad was planning on moving and probably hadn't shown up because he was avoiding having the difficult conversation.

Bean called me in tears. When we got off the phone, I called Dave myself to ask him what in the world was keeping him from loving this absolutely perfect daughter that he was so lucky to have. This dumb-ass man responded by reciting a laundry list of all the ways life had been unfair to him, one of those being that his mom hadn't given him any money for his birthday that year. *Girl*, your mom doesn't need to give you money, she needs to give you a swift kick in your ass.

After expressing his woes, Dave told me that he had to focus on himself. I responded the only way I could, which was to tell Dave that he was a terrible dad. He laughed and asked me what I knew about being a father. "I may not have had a child of my own, but I'm raising yours," I said before hanging up on him.

Later that week I called Bean to see how she was doing. She told me that she had spent a lot of time thinking about the situation with her dad and had decided to let him go. Once she made that decision, she told him that she wanted him to go to Tennessee because he was clearly struggling with his life in Florida. She told him that she loved him, but she also needed him to leave for her own well-being.

"You will always be my dad," Bean said to Dave, "and I will always love you. But I can't carry the pain you cause me while you figure out what being my dad means." *What!?* Socrates who? I was left speechless by the depth and wisdom of this child.

Bean went on to explain to me that she understands her dad acts the way he does not because he doesn't love her, but because he doesn't love himself. She told me she can have empathy for why he makes the choices that he does, but that doesn't mean she has to accept them.

Through my tears I told Bean just how proud of her I was. Not just for coming to this profound realization, but also for maintaining her positivity and joy despite the ways she's had to fight through life. That girl is the strongest person I know.

Bean's wisdom and elegance made me stop and evaluate how I was dealing with tricky relationships in my own life. It allowed me the opportunity to consider the fact that sometimes I can redefine how much access someone has to me, rather than completely shutting the relationship down forever.

Your work for this part of your journey is very personal to you. I want you to think about some of the relationships in your life that feel heavy as you are journaling, and I want you to consider whether it feels like they need to be demolished or simply renovated.

Here's what evaluating them can look like:

- *Identify the relationships.* Who feels painful or confusing in your life?
- *Get honest with yourself.* What do you wish that person would do or be for you? How do you feel after interacting with them?
- *Name your truth.* Can you accept this person as they are without expecting any more? Would that still be honoring yourself?
- *Set your boundary path.* Do you need to release this relationship? It can be with love, not hate, and you can hope for the best for them. Do you want them to stay in your life, but where you set new roles and rules?

As you get more and more experience standing up for yourself, remember that there can be balance and nuance. You can maintain your compassion for the people in your world while also refusing to allow them to negatively impact you.

Whether you need to kick someone to the curb, let them end things, or enter a new era where a relationship doesn't look the same way it always has, I hope you are proud of the person you've become as you stand your ground for yourself and move forward in your life with a refined sense of self-preservation that is kind yet fierce.

She told me she can have empathy for why he makes the choices that he does, but that doesn't mean she has to accept them.

—Part IV—

SCULPT THE LIFE YOU WANT

You've done the work, Bestie. You've dug deep, stood tall, and maybe cried a little—or a lot—along the way. But that brings us to the best part of being sassy: sculpting the life you actually want. This is where you stop settling for whatever life throws your way and instead start shaping your reality with intention. You can let the world chip away at you until you're unrecognizable, or you can pick up the damn chisel and carve out the masterpiece that makes you proud.

This is where you reclaim every piece of yourself that you've lost along the way. Maybe you've poured so much love into others that you forgot to save any for yourself. Maybe you spent too many years trying to win over people who were never going to cheer for you. Maybe you've clung to an outdated version of yourself and never gave yourself permission to grow. Well, Bestie, that stops today. Rewrites are allowed and dreams should be so big they scare people. And if someone has a problem with you taking up space like some guy manspreading in the seat next to you on an airplane—*good*! That means you're finally doing it right.

At the end of the day, the life you want isn't going to build itself. But now you finally have the tools to know how to build it yourself.

Surround yourself with people who lift you up, chase the dreams that make your heart race, and remember that you are the main character of this story. *Your* story.

So let's get to it. Audacity is on sale, and you can finally afford to create an extraordinary life for yourself—one so bold, so beautiful, and so *you* that the world can't help but stop every time you pass a mirror and think, *Daaaaaaaaamn. I'm* that *bitch!*

CHAPTER 16

MIRROR, MIRROR ON THE WALL, WHO'S THE SASSIEST OF THEM ALL?

Hey, Bestie! Have you ever felt like you were fading into the background of your own life, putting everyone else first and calling it love? I sure have. But, Bestie, I promise that taking care of yourself isn't selfish. The fullest, happiest version of you is the person who the people you love *deserve* to see.

The thing is, we don't disappear all at once. It's a quiet, gradual descent. It happens as we are busy becoming parents, employees, partners, and every other label we get slapped with in life, trying our best to live up to their expectations. And then it all sticks and we let them shape us. Somewhere along the way we start to believe that love means giving up what we need, that being good often means coming last. The thing is, though, Bestie, one day you'll wake up and look in the mirror and wonder, "Where the hell did I go?"

I truly believe that one of the biggest reasons why my marriage works is because we never stopped being two separate people.

Okay, that might not sound romantic, but it's the truth. I think that a lot of us have fallen into the trap of chasing the fantasy of love—the dream of an all-consuming kind of togetherness where we are finishing each other's sentences and never spending one second apart, making everyone around us throw up in disgust. That had been the goal in most of my past relationships. But what I've learned, and what has kept me from murdering my husband, is that closeness without boundaries is exhausting.

When my husband and I were dating, especially after we moved in together, we hit a little rough patch. It wasn't some dramatic betrayal or toxic pattern. Just a little friction. Irritation. And things started to become a little claustrophobic. I know that I was feeling stir-crazy and frustrated. He was feeling drained and cornered. There was one random Tuesday night when he came home from work to me sitting there waiting for him, and I immediately greeted him with grenades of, "Where do you want to go for dinner?," "There's a spin class I've been wanting to go to, should we go tonight?" And I'll never forget the way he looked at me with this expression like I was a lizard person, before he shouted, "I'M NOT YOUR ENTERTAINMENT COMMITTEE!" He had never yelled at me before, so I was shocked. But then we started uncontrollably laughing.

We realized in that moment that we were trying to live too closely. Not emotionally, but literally. Like physically. Constantly. Every night, every errand, every meal was together. But I'm someone who needs to be around people and get out into the world. Constant motion. He's someone who loves being home, recharging in peace. He can spend five hours alone in a room and be totally content. I'll spend five hours alone in a room and start speaking to the plants.

We had slowly been giving up the things that recharged us, thinking that we had to give them up for each other. I was turning down the things I wanted to do to wait and do them with him because I was being a "good partner." He was tagging along to everything I ever wanted to do because that was "quality time." What we were really doing was making ourselves, and each other, tired and resentful.

It was such a valuable lesson for me. I was used to the unhealthy relationships of my past, so I thought this was normal. We didn't need more time together—we needed more time to be ourselves. I needed to say, "Hey, I love you, but I'm going to go do this thing that makes me feel like a human again and you don't need to come." I got to go out to dinner with friends, and he got to stay home and watch a documentary about Big Foot that I had zero interest in. These little breaks weirdly brought us back to each other.

Now we don't try to be everything to each other. Love doesn't mean 24/7 access. I know he loves me even if he's not sitting on the couch next to me. He knows I love him even if I open a book as soon as I hear anything paranormal on the TV. And for us, that has made all the difference.

I think a lot of us fall into this pattern. Not just in our romantic relationships but with anyone we hold dear. We start to believe that in order to be a good partner, parent, or friend, we have to be available and perfect all the time. And before we know it, we have lost touch with the parts of ourselves that make us feel like we even exist.

Which brings me to my friend Melissa. Mel and I met through social media. She was a follower of mine and sent me a message offering restaurant recommendations I might need when I posted I was moving to Austin, Texas. (Pro tip: If you want to immediately become my best friend, put good food in my belly.)

Mel and I chatted via DM for a couple of months and discovered we have quite a bit in common: We're close in age, we like a lot of the same activities, like hiking, we both love our dogs, and her restaurant recs didn't disappoint. We took our friendship offline when Mel asked if I wanted to meet up for a coffee. Being new to the city, I was happy to make a friend!

Mel and I met at one of her favorite coffee shops (another home run pick from her!), and we proceeded to have a great afternoon. She was funny, sincere, and had a mouth like a sailor. I was fucking sold.

One of my favorite things about Mel was how she lit up when she talked about her family. She is married to a unicorn of a man named Alex, who even *I* have a crush on because he is so beautifully loving toward her. Alex and Mel had recently welcomed their first baby, Emma, who was fast approaching her first birthday.

While sipping our overpriced cortados, Mel said to me, "I hope we can be real friends, but I'm afraid I've become that boring mom." She paused for a moment before continuing, "Hey! You should have a kid so we can have playdates."

I chuckled but didn't make much of Mel's comment. I mean, how often have you made a self-deprecating joke about being a parent? Even if you're not a parent yourself, I'm willing to bet you know someone who's always cracking a joke about how their whole life revolves around their kids. It's super normal, right?

Over the next few months, I met up with Mel just a couple more times because she was so busy. The second time we met up, I got to meet her hunk of a husband, Alex, as well as little Emma—let me tell you, they are a gorge family. Over lunch, Mel apologized that it had been so long since we had last hung out and lamented that she wasn't "more fun."

Alex interjected, insisting that she should make more of a point to go out and do her own thing. She just shrugged and said, "Maybe in eighteen years."

Again, at the time, none of these comments raised any red flags for me when Mel said them. She was always smiling and delivered the lines with a goofy eye roll and a laugh. And again, it's not abnormal to hear parents—and especially moms—say things like this. Something I've come to learn from loving so many women and from having so many women touch my life is that the sudden shift from "me" to "mom" can be overwhelming. And Mel was definitely feeling that.

It was Alex who brought it to my attention that there was actually something there, even if Mel was trying to play it cool. After our lunch, he sent me a message saying that even though Mel would never tell me this, she had followed me on social media because she wasn't feeling great about herself and needed a confidence boost. He shared that she often watched my videos and commented that she wished she felt that good about herself.

"Why can't I be more like Misha?" she would ask. He told me that she was putting on a brave face for the world but struggling with depression behind the scenes.

Alex asked if I would help. He wanted me to ask Mel out for a spa day on him so that she could spend a day getting pampered. He didn't think she would ever go if he just gave her a gift card, but he thought she would commit if she had a friend to go with. He was hopeful this would give her a bit of the boost she needed. Of course, I said yes! I mean, who the hell turns down helping out a friend while having a free day at the spa at the same time? Count me in!

Alex booked us for the following Saturday, and he went *all* out. We had facials, a "couple's" massage, and a manicure! (I *told* you that Alex is the kind of man you want to drop your panties for, ha!) Mel and I had our massage first, which was so relaxing. Then we had two hours to kill before our facial, so we wandered over to a cabana by the resort pool, where we finally had a chance to chat.

"I miss this version of Mel," she said, leaning back and letting out a big exhale.

This was my moment! "I don't think that being a mom has to be a funeral for your former self," I replied.

Mel looked at me and seemed to be trying to laugh, but instead she emitted a guttural noise as her face contorted and she started to cry. I watched her try to hold it in, but it was too late and her pent-up feelings came pouring out.

I listened for the next hour as Mel talked about how it felt like she was going through an identity crisis as she adjusted to motherhood because she found herself comparing her own feelings to the perfect Instagram moms who seemed to lose themselves in their kids. She felt a lot of Mom Guilt about the fact that she had found it difficult to connect with Emma in those first few months because of her postpartum depression. Now she spent all her time and energy overcompensating by trying to be the best mom she possibly could.

Even though her doctors, therapist, husband, and friends told her that she had nothing to feel guilty about, Mel got stuck in a shame spiral about the fact that the happiest event of her life had caused her so much guilt. Mel is a lover and giver. All she wants is to consider what her baby needs, what her husband needs. And she wasn't able to show up for them in the way that she wanted. Even if they understood, it wasn't good enough for her. Then Mel asked me, "Do you think I'm a bad mom?"

With the most sincerity I could muster, I said, *"Absolutely not!"*

Bestie, I'm saying this to you as well: Believe it or not, there are people out there who don't even care if they are a good parent. So if you care, you're ahead of the curve already.

I asked Mel if she felt good being at the spa, despite the fact that she had a snot bubble coming out of her nose as she cried. When she nodded, I told her that spa days feel good because we know we're doing something just for ourselves. Bestie, I want you to hear this too: *Self-care is not selfish, it's self-preservation.*

"Mel," I asked, "if you lose all sense of who you are, what would that be teaching Emma? That self-sacrifice is the only way to love? That others' needs always need to come before her own? You're not just raising a kid; you're raising a future adult."

Mel laughed and brushed her tears away, and the two of us proceeded to spend the remainder of the day luxuriating. As we walked back to our cars post-manicure, she told me how the day had been so necessary and that she felt recharged. She smiled and said she felt more like herself than she had in a while. I reminded Mel that I am a bougie bitch and *always* down for a self-care day, so I was expecting another one very soon—next time on me, of course.

You know I will always keep it real with you, Bestie, so I have to tell you that this one day did not fix all of Mel's problems. She went home to a baby that needed her and a life that still expected a lot more out of her. Even with her strong (and sexy) support system, it's still a lot.

The routine of day-to-day life can be really good at putting its nasty little claws in us and keeping us stuck in a cycle that isn't necessarily good for us. That was just as true for Mel as it is for all of us.

Alex must have noticed the relief Mel felt that night after the spa because he didn't allow her to linger in that vicious cycle for too long. He insisted she understand that while she would always have a responsibility to their daughter and life would always put an ever-growing list of expectations on her, she needed to incorporate some sassy self-care in there as well. She needed to remember who she was and to hold on to all the parts of herself—even (if not especially) the parts that didn't revolve around being a mom.

A few weeks later, I texted my new spa buddy to ask if she wanted to meet up for our next day of letting some tiny but feral woman beat our bodies for an hour, and I was pleasantly surprised when she said yes. Well, what she actually said was, "Alex will kill me if I don't go."

When I asked Mel how she was doing, she told me that she was doing better but still wished that she were more like me. Bestie, *no*! I reminded Mel that I don't have a child, I have gone through my own shit, and that for as much as I think I am the bomb.com, if the world were full of Mishas, then I wouldn't be special. What Mel needed to be was Mel. And this was her opportunity to relearn who *she* was and figure out the balance between being Supermom and a badass woman who makes herself feel the best she can.

I'm happy to report that I've had a lot of bestie days with Mel since then. She is still doing what women do best: multitasking. But today she's remembering the entire-ass person she was before she became a mom and realizing that there is a new version of that person available to her. Having Emma was an addition to her life, not an erasure of who Mel was as an individual. It has been a beautiful experience to watch someone who has such a big heart learn to use that heart to love on herself. The facials are nice too.

Bestie, this is me giving you permission to be a person. Reclaim who you are beneath the role.

Here's your homework: I want you to go back to a time before you had all the responsibilities that come with the roles you play. What did you love to do? What did you dream of? Does any of that still apply? I want you to map out, even schedule, time that is just for you. It can be time to recharge, time to put some energy into your own desires, or time to lean on your support systems and do a little delegating.

This can feel a lot like the time you spent with yourself when we were working on your affirmations, where you forgot all your outside responsibilities and just focused on what would build you up. But this is more than that. The time spent on yourself here can include work, even self-improvement that isn't necessarily fun. Whatever it is, you have to stand your ground. Stop trying to do everything for everyone, and start focusing on what helps you grow.

Other people can hold everything together to give you a few hours to yourself. My friend Mel had a whole-ass husband willing to help, and she's learning that he can take a little bit of her load off her shoulders. This is your time to reconnect with yourself as an individual who deserves the same kind of love you pour into others.

As you start sculpting the life you want, here's your reminder that you are not just what life demands of you—you are who *you* choose to be. Whether you are a parent or child-free, loud as hell or a quiet force, the life of the party or queen of the cozy corner, you deserve to exist as the fullest version of yourself.

Your happiness isn't a luxury, it's your right. Own it, protect it, and most importantly, Bestie, live it.

“The fullest, happiest version of you is the person who the people you love deserve to see.”

CHAPTER 17

QUEENS SUPPORT QUEENS

Hey, Bestie! You've done a great job of reprioritizing yourself, and I do believe that the most important relationship in your life is your relationship with yourself. But for as much as you are the main character in your own story, I hope that as you flourish, you will spread that love to others—particularly to the people who believe in and support you on your good and bad days alike. I truly think that you get back what you put out into the world.

Bestie, you know that if you came to me and told me you just got that promotion you've been fighting for at work, I would celebrate just as hard, if not harder, than if it were me who was promoted. If you support your people, hopefully they will have your back just as enthusiastically. (And if not, please see Chapter 7 for further instructions.)

Speaking of queens supporting queens, as they should, I want to tell you about one of my best friends, Jennifer. Jen is one of my musical theatre buds from college. We met when I transferred to SUNY Fredonia my junior year. Jen was a freshman, but because we arrived at the school the same year, we were put in the same theatre classes. I was already fully in my naughty boy era, partying as hard and as often as I could. Jen, on the other hand, was still channeling her role as Belle in her high school's production of *Beauty and the Beast*, which made total sense because Jen was literally a Disney princess come to life. She was slightly awkward in a gloriously endearing way, dripping with pure talent, and so innocent that her very essence basically screamed "I'm a good girl!" The two of us didn't make any sense as best friends.

And yet, despite our respective bad boy and good girl personas, we became inseparable. Wherever there was Misha, there was Jen, and wherever there was Jen, you could be sure Misha was belting out some showtune behind her. Thanks to my fantastic and ever-present influence, it wasn't long before Jen was taking elective courses in Beer Pong 101 and Smoking Pot: Is it a Gateway Drug?, both taught by yours truly. Within several weeks, everybody knew that if the two of us were together (which we usually were), we were probably up to no good.

There was one incident where the theatre department faculty was going to hold a program-wide meeting. At first there were so many excited whispers about what the meeting was going to be about. Was the theatre getting a revamp? Was some Broadway star coming to speak to us? Was that one acting teacher who was married but sleeping with one of the girls in the junior class finally going to address the scandal? Well, no, it wasn't as juicy as that.

Rumors and gossip did what they do best and leaked that this congregation of drama queens was for the purpose of the teachers chastising the students for the amount of partying we were doing. They knew we were doing drugs. They knew we were having wild off-campus parties even on random Tuesday nights.

While most of my peers were horrified that their bad behavior wasn't a secret to the teachers they held in such high regard, I couldn't have cared less. And in my immature defiance, I suggested to Jen that we get high before the meeting. That would show them. We did follow through with that idea, but even a bunch of teenagers who were known pot smokers thought it was disrespectful.

Unlike many other relationships that involve a lot of drinking and drugging, Jen and I really loved each other. It wasn't a situation of convenience or codependence. No, we were truly the best of friends. Case in point: One time we went to a friend's house to hang out. This particular friend wasn't one of those college kids who just smokes weed and chugs beer. He was the kind of guy who would do ayahuasca and then go live in the woods for two months. That particular night, our drug connoisseur friend asked if we had ever tried salvia.

I told him that I had and thought it was a waste of money—in my experience salvia was some random "drug" you could buy at a gas station. Our friend informed me that he was talking about *real* salvia—from his parents who had gone down to Mexico.

Jen looked at me nervously, and I told her not to worry—I would go first. I put my mouth to the bong and inhaled like the pro that I was. The next thing I remember is waking up on the living room floor with everyone standing around me, as Jen cried and asked if I was okay, while looking absolutely terrified.

Apparently, I took the bong hit, exhaled, and immediately fell forward onto the floor as my eyes rolled into the back of my head and I started convulsing. While on the ground, I yelled, "Jen, RUN!" My friends were all shaking me in an attempt to snap me out of it, but I was gone. The entire event lasted less than a minute.

As I recalibrated to the universe over the course of the next couple of hours back in the comfort of my dorm room, I slowly started to remember little bits and pieces of what I had just experienced. I remembered that in the midst of my drug-induced travel, I felt fear as I had never before experienced in my life. I believed that I had entered a new plane of existence where I lost myself completely and would never get myself back. The only other thing I remembered was how important it felt to me that Jen *not* take the salvia and suffer the same fate. And I never forgot that feeling of wanting to protect Jen.

I wasn't the only person who wanted to protect Jen from my bad choices. Later that year I was pulled into the head of the theatre department's office. He told me that everyone knew I was a bad influence and "corrupting Jennifer," as he put it, probably because I got her high before that meeting. He put me on probation and said that I needed to turn my behavior around and wouldn't be allowed to perform in any shows the next semester. In response, I did what I always did when confronted with accountability or criticism back then: I quit. Instead of returning to SUNY the following year, I moved to New York City to pursue my dreams and get my life started.

Three years later, Jen moved to the big city with the same hopes and dreams that all of us aspiring actors have. But shortly after she arrived, I started booking work that took me away from the city—and, before long, Jen booked a tour herself.

One day while Jen was out on tour, she sent me a message that wasn't overly dramatic or emotional but still stopped me in my tracks. Her simple and raw message said, "I don't think I'm happy. I might want to quit." I could feel her hesitancy through the screen like she was bracing for me to be disappointed in her.

Toxic positivity often makes people respond by telling you that you've come this far so don't quit now. But that's not what came out. I told her, "Whatever makes you happy, I support." Because I meant it. The tour wasn't going to be her big break, and it definitely wasn't the dream either of us had. If she was miserable, I wanted her off that bus.

But it turned out that she wasn't just talking about the tour. She opened up, and it came out in one long vulnerable message. She was unhappy with everything. The gigs, the constant moving, the stretches of loneliness in hotel rooms and dressing rooms. She missed feeling grounded. Missed her family. She missed herself.

With a sort of finality, she told me that she was going to leave the tour and move back home. And just like that, our old dream of sharing an apartment in New York City, chasing the bright lights and stages of Broadway, was just poof . . . gone. I'd be lying to you if I said it didn't hurt. Not because I didn't support her, but because I wasn't good at accepting that the people we were at 18 years old were evolving. And sometimes evolving means you have to let go.

But my own selfish reasons for wanting her to keep going didn't mean I thought she was making a mistake or failing in any way. And I had to make that clear because I knew Jen wasn't just afraid of quitting, but of letting me down. A huge part of me felt like I had to show my support for her because I was once the person who had dragged her into some really questionable situations back in college. I had pulled her into the party because I didn't want to be alone, and we ended up platonically falling in love with each other, and now here she was pulling herself out of something that didn't feel right. There was no way I was going to be anything but a cheerleader. Real friendship doesn't mourn someone else's growth, even if it means we grow apart.

Over the next few years, Jen and I reunited for a night here and there when she came to New York for a visit. But that wasn't often. For Jen and me, months—and at one point, even a couple of years—would go by between our visits. No matter how long it had been, though, we always picked up exactly where we left off. Time and distance didn't matter to us.

Eventually, Jen built her own life at home in upstate New York, while I was off traveling the world on cruise ships. Our own disparate circumstances were exacerbated by the fact that a lot of our college friends had also moved out of the city or otherwise slowly drifted away, which meant there were fewer and fewer get-togethers of any kind to be had.

But over the years, we managed to celebrate each other's birthdays, accomplishments, and anything and everything else good that has happened. We chatted about what was going on in our lives—and even if those conversations were only occasional during certain periods of time, we never let our flame burn out completely. After a while, our paths started to run parallel to each other, even though our lives looked different in so many ways.

These parallel paths included our relationship with alcohol. When I got sober, Jen was one of the first people I talked to about it. I remember seeing her words on my phone, "I'm proud of you." No judgment, just support. Not long into my sobriety, Jen messaged me and said that she was thinking about her own relationship with drinking too. And while I was bursting into my own journey with clarity and momentum, Jen was still sitting in the place where you are shouting inside your head because you're too afraid to shout out loud. It would take her two more years to step into her own sobriety.

As a true testament of how ride-or-die Jen is, during those two years she still managed to show up for me, even if her own life felt unsteady. Every milestone I hit—30 days, 90 days, one whole freaking year—she was there for me. She celebrated these milestones as if they were her own. She never let her own pain turn into bitterness or envy. There was never a time she made me feel like I needed to make space for her discomfort. This kind of love is rare, and this is a friendship you should cling to like your damn life depends on it.

Bestie, I have to be honest. I have had to come to terms with feelings of guilt that I was a bad influence on Jen in college. I was older, more experienced with drugs and alcohol than she was, and I think she looked up to me in a lot of ways. I wish that I could go back and slap my younger self in the face and warn him to look after little Jen better. But, of course, I can't.

What I *can* do is take any chance I get to remind her that I look up to her. I look up to her as the woman who has reinvented herself more than once because she knew what she needed. I look up to her because her heart is so big, and she is capable of giving so much love to others, even in the moments when she can't care for herself in the same way. Jen is such a safe space for those who are lucky enough to be loved by her that she even helped me stop running in reaction to feeling like I was "bad." Because that's what I did in the past when I was faced with criticism or accountability, I ran. Being confronted with how my choices may have affected other people was uncomfortable (and by "uncomfortable," I mean I wanted to get sucked into a black hole and cease to exist). But Jen never flinched. She stood by me through it all, through sobriety, and reminded me without ever needing to say it, that there was goodness in me that was worth sticking around for. Even when I was an immature asshole. Even when I was a reckless tornado.

Jen is worth doing the hard work for. And I'm so glad I did because it's been such a beautiful experience to cheer on these new versions of each other, so opposite from who we each were when we met. I don't have words for how proud I am of Jen for her determination and strength in reclaiming herself. She's truly an inspiration.

Our lives have mirrored each other's in other ways too. Jen became a beast at the gym and, ultimately, a fitness instructor. In my sobriety, I have also become very passionate about fitness. I was even certified as a personal trainer during COVID. Jen continued to perform, doing many independent films over the years, as well as community theatre. I obviously continued to perform on those damned ships, in theatres across the country, and with Cirque.

Then at the end of 2023, I was approached to participate in a new reality TV show. It was a singing competition that required contestants to have another person with them to act as a support system. I immediately thought of Jen, who has never been quiet in her support of me, celebrating me through every chapter of my life without hesitation. Of course she would be the perfect support system for all of America to witness! When I told the producers we hadn't seen each other in *10 years*, they started salivating at the thought of an on-screen reunion.

Jen and I each made it through many rounds of interviews, signed contracts and nondisclosure agreements, and were basically told that we were just waiting for a filming date to be set. This whole experience really reignited our friendship because we were now talking about this new opportunity all the time. Unfortunately, the show never happened and we didn't get that chance to have our big reunion for all of America to see. But a reunion was still going to happen—we were bound and determined.

Well, wouldn't you know that another parallel track in our lives was that we were both about to get married? Jen met the love of her life, John, waaaaaaaaaay back in her New York City days, and they have been together ever since. Of course, I, on the other hand, went through liars, cheaters, and idiots before finding my husband. One day, Jen sent me a video of herself blubbering like a baby. She was in the thick of planning her wedding and explained that she had always envisioned me being a part of her wedding day. Then she asked me to sing a song for her and John's first dance.

A few weeks later, I saw my very best friend walk down the aisle to marry the person who has cared for her as well as anyone I could have hoped for. There weren't television cameras and producers surrounding us, and honestly, I'm really glad it worked out the way that it did. I share so much of my life with the world, and it felt really special to have a private moment of celebration.

While all the guests were mingling at the cocktail reception as the newly bound families were having their pictures taken, I slipped out of the endless, "So how do you know Jen?" conversations because I had consumed about 38 sparkling waters and really needed the bathroom. As I stepped into the hallway, I ran into Jen. Tears immediately swelled in both of our eyes, and she ran to me and gave me a massive hug. And let me tell you, bitch, it hurt because she has legit muscles now.

Shortly after our long-anticipated reunion, it was time for me to sing "Anywhere for You" by the Backstreet Boys as Jen had requested

(#bsbforever). I have performed on television, on radio, in front of presidents of whole-ass countries, and onstage in front of 18,000 people without batting a single eyelash. But I was nervous for this. I wanted the song to be perfect for them, but I also didn't want to upstage my best friend and her husband.

I took the microphone from the DJ and walked to the corner of the dance floor. I blew Jen a kiss and started to sing. At first my voice was shaky because the lump in my throat was practically choking me. I was brimming over with happiness that Jen was so happy that I almost turned into a puddle all over the floor. John made Jen laugh as the two of them swayed across the dance floor, and I felt deeply comforted knowing that she was taken care of.

For nearly 18 years now, Jen has been a loud and vocal supporter of my career(s), my sobriety, and, most recently, my new adventure as a husband. Through all the noise of being let down by others, Jen has reminded me of how hard we have both worked for everything we have today. She is the kind of person you want to cheer on, and she is the kind of person who makes you feel loved, even from 1,500 miles away.

There's no way I would write a book and not include someone who has been there and supported me through every stage of my life, from creeping around campus, to being a show pony on cruise ships, to being an Internet celebrity. Jen has never stopped telling me that she's proud of me, that I'm making a difference, and that she always believed I'm destined for great things. Same, girl, same!

Looking back, I realize how easy it would have been for her to drift away. But she never did. Instead, she clapped the loudest for me. And when she was finally ready to take her own first steps into sobriety, her career, and her marriage, I have been able to return the favor. So I'm here to remind her of the very same thing she once told me: I'm proud of you.

Who do you have in your life that cheers you on? Here's what I want you to do:

- *Figure out who those ride-or-dies are.* Who are the friends that celebrate you without competition? Who can be happy for you even if they are struggling? What bestie makes you feel safe?
- *Reflect on their love.* How have they shown their support for you and how did that impact you? What is it about them that makes the love feel unconditional?
- *Be a mirror.* Bestie, reflect that shit right back at them. I want you to pull out your phone and call them or send them a text to randomly tell them you are proud of them. Seriously, it can seem cheesy, but it can be a huge gesture. Really listen to them when they are leaning on you for support or needing advice. Celebrate the pants off them just as they would for you.

So, Bestie, as you come into your own and experience the colossal shift—or, more likely, shifts—that comes with it, keep the friends like Jen close, the friends who equally support all versions of you. It is so easy to focus on the people who try with all their might to keep you shackled where you are. But letting go of their expectations of you and their desire to keep you small in order to make themselves feel bigger and instead choosing to be like Jen, and to love people like Jen, will make being great all the more delicious.

Part of the joy and the reward of sculpting the life you want is choosing the people you want to be a part of it. Choose wisely.

"She clapped the loudest for me. And when she was finally ready to take her own first steps into sobriety, her career, and her marriage, I have been able to return the favor."

CHAPTER 18

REWRITES ARE ALLOWED

Hey, Bestie! You know what seems like it would be exhausting? Holding on to the person you once were to keep other people comfortable—or even to keep yourself comfortable. It's easy to cling to a previous version of yourself because it's familiar, even when it no longer fits.

Could you imagine still rocking a side ponytail or, even worse, believing low-rise jeans are your only option? No judgment here, Bestie, but . . . evolution. Growth isn't betrayal, changing your mind isn't weakness, and expanding your worldview doesn't mean the old you was a total f-ing idiot. It just means you've learned some things. And isn't that the whole point? You don't still use a flip phone because they're outdated (if you still have a flip phone, don't come for me—you're still valid!). So why would you hold on to outdated opinions?

I've heard from so many besties—both online and in person—that my stories have been a sort of permission slip for them to pivot, evolve, and rewrite parts of their own story that no longer fit who they are or what they want. In this chapter, I want to share three of those stories that perfectly demonstrate how, sometimes, part of sculpting the life you want means ensuring that your past doesn't hold your future hostage.

One day I went to the nail salon to get a mani. I had seen some chrome nails that I thought looked cool and was determined to get a set of my own. If you're one of my OG followers, you know that when I used to frequent the nail salon, I had some pretty unsavory encounters with closed-minded people who didn't know how to keep their opinions to themselves. But on this particular day, everything was going smoothly.

As I chatted with the nail technician, she asked me what I did for work. When I said that I was a social media celebrity, an older woman next to us exclaimed, "Oh, my god! I thought that was you. I follow you!"

This woman and I chatted for a few minutes before she got up to wash her hands and pay. Before leaving the salon, she came back over and said that it had been nice to meet me and chat. Of course I didn't let her leave before showering her with compliments on her Easter purple sparkly nails because *yaaaassss,* queen!

When I got up to pay a little later, the girl behind the desk told me that the woman I had been speaking with had paid for my nails. Not only that, but she had also handed the girl a handwritten note to give to me. This is what it said:

> *I really need to thank you for what you do. You probably don't remember this, but I messaged you about a year ago because my grandson came out as gay. I couldn't believe you answered me and were so gracious. This is very embarrassing for me, but most of my life I was the kind of person you make your videos about. I grew up in a small town in Texas. I was homophobic and intolerant of people different than people I know. I started watching you because I thought you were hysterical, but the more I watched, the more I realized that you care about people you don't even know—people who are different from you. It made me think about why my own worldview was so small, and I wanted to change that.*

It makes me sad to this day to think how I could have disowned my own grandson because of who he is. Paying for some silly nail polish doesn't seem like enough. Watching your videos saved my family. Thank you.

Bestie, can you imagine if I had stopped making my content when that one celebrity marched her way into my direct messages to tell me I was doing it wrong!? Like, what if she made me second-guess what I was doing and I started making cooking videos instead? No shade to those creators, love that stuff too! But how different could this grandma's relationship with her grandson have been?

The thing is, I may have been the catalyst for her to change, but she was ultimately the one who did the heavy lifting. She had to face herself, probably her family, probably her whole damn community, and admit that what they believed was wrong. That's not easy to do at any age, but particularly when you've believed something to be true for as long as she had. It's an impressive feat to be able to grow and not feel like you are attacking your previous self in the process.

The thing that punched me right in the gut about this woman was realizing how much pain she (and her grandson) avoided because she was able to honestly reflect on and take accountability for her upbringing. Thanks to her accountability, bravery, and willingness to evolve, her family is able to experience life without the huge conflict or split that could have been. She said that she was embarrassed for the things she used to believe, but I hope that over time, the pride she feels every day for loving her grandson for who he is will far outweigh that guilt.

For more proof that you can change your life at any age, I want to tell you about an older man named Henry who followed me. One day I was checking my direct messages and came across this:

My name is Henry and you have really helped me. You see, I am almost 82 years old, and I have spent the last 20 or so years only a shell of the man I once was. I had a partner named Doug, who I met in the military, and he was the love of my life for 42 years. He left me 20 years ago for Ronnie, some little boy toy, and that's when my life stopped.

As sad as it is, I have allowed Doug and Ronnie to live in my dead sister's house all these years because I hoped Doug would love me again. My niece showed me your page a while ago and I started learning about your sassy ways. I don't much like the profanity, but your heart is in the right place. Turns out, a couple of days ago, I decided enough was enough. I told Doug that I was going to sell the house and use the money to go on some cruises before I get too old. He told me I was selfish and jealous and childish. But I looked him right in his eye and said, "Corinthians 13: When I was a child, I spake as a child, I understood as a child, I thought as a child. But when I became a man, I put away childish things." And then I made one of your sassy looks in Ronnie's direction. Oh, he was so mad! But that was the first time I stuck up for myself like that to him and I thought I would share that with you. You really are like a friend.

I bawled my eyes out when I read that message. I felt my own heart break as I fully sat with the idea of letting people walk all over you like a doormat because you hope that *one day* you will be chosen again.

I chatted with Henry a little bit, and he was so angry at himself for wasting so many years. I reminded him that even though he may have put too much energy into someone who didn't deserve it, loving someone with your whole heart is never a bad thing. A lot of people could learn something about loyalty and devotion from Henry. But what I really wanted him to focus on was that it was okay to forgive himself for putting Doug first in the past and to intentionally choose himself moving forward.

But before I move on from the total badass—sorry bad*butt*—that is Henry, I want to let you know that Henry did, in fact, go on that cruise. A few months later, he sent me a photo of himself on the ship, where he was living his best life. Doug and Ronnie were out on their butts, while Henry got to go on the kind of adventure he had only dreamed of up to that point—all because he chose to write a new story and put himself first. Henry can teach us all that just because we've always been one way, it doesn't mean we have to stay that way.

The last story I want to share with you is actually quite similar to the first but, unfortunately, the difference is that the pain wasn't avoided this time. I got this message from one of my followers after she watched my story about catching the nasty-ass pedo in the pet store:

> *My dearest Misha,*
>
> *I hope you see this. I will try to be quick. My family has been broken for the past 12 years. When my son came out as gay, my husband banned him from the house and my son moved on with his life.*
>
> *I found you a few months ago, from a video where you were talking about the lady you take to church. I was shocked that a gay person would do that because we don't see that where I live. I have watched all your videos since then. Sometimes I don't agree, but I still "like" all of them.*
>
> *Well, I watch videos with the sound on, so my husband has heard all of them from his chair, and sometimes says, "That guy's funny." But you changed him. The other day, he said you were a stand-up guy for talking about the men who follow children's [social media] accounts, and he said, "I would be proud if that were my kid." Misha, I have never seen my husband cry—not even when his parents died—but he did then. It hit him like a ton of bricks that maybe he does have that kid.*

She went on to share that she told her husband she was tired of having a fractured family and he needed to reach out to their son. After a few more conversations, he *did* contact their estranged son and told him they were so sorry for how they had reacted to his coming out. Eventually, their son agreed to come home so they could talk face-to-face, and the woman who wrote to me said that it was a good start to getting their relationship back.

The one thing that really stood out to me was when she told me that her son also apologized to them. He said that he hadn't reached out in all the time that they were estranged because of the way he lashed out when their conflict initially happened. He felt guilty about the things that he'd said and was afraid they wouldn't want to speak to him again.

My observation is that they were all holding on to past versions of themselves, and by doing so, they allowed shame and guilt to keep them away from each other. But when they found the bravery to confront their past, they found a path forward, even if it's just a start. And now they have something they haven't had in a long time: hope.

Something I would like to point out is that I told each of these stories on social media when they happened and got a ton of praise for each of them. But I think that personal praise was wildly misdirected. I can share my stories, give my opinions, and lead by example all I want, but if these people hadn't had the fortitude and desire to *hear* what I'm sharing, *reflect* on how it applies to them, and *take action*, then it wouldn't mean anything. Along with so many other people I've heard from over the years, the people whose stories I've shared here are doing the work—they're taking charge of their own lives, evaluating what's not working, and making a conscious decision to change.

Growth isn't just some buzzword for all of us therapy girlies; it's a real, tangible thing that can change lives. These stories aren't just about opinions changing; they're about people stepping into bigger, fuller versions of themselves. A woman chose love over old beliefs. A man chose freedom over false hope. A family chose healing over pride. They all rewrote their stories in ways they probably couldn't have imagined . . . until they actually did it.

The best part? You can too.

If you've been clinging to an old version of yourself because it's all you've ever known or because it's comfortable, consider this a flashing neon sign to let that shit go. Listen, I understand that marinating in your own shit becomes oddly comfortable and that the thought of getting out of that briny concoction can feel scary. But I am forever an optimist (so fucking annoying, I know!), and I think there is so much value in seeing the opportunities a new future offers. New experiences, learning things about yourself you never knew before, loving people you previously wouldn't have ever known, and so much more could fill that space you create by expanding beyond what you currently know and believe.

Now it is your turn. This can be tough, but I want you to remember that you don't owe your past self shit, except maybe the opportunity to grow. Here is your task:

- *Sit in the feelings of a moment where your past choices or beliefs now make your stomach flip and your heart sink.* Maybe you hurt someone, you had a belief you've outgrown, or you stayed silent when you should have spoken up. Just be honest with yourself, even if it is uncomfortable.

- *Ask yourself the hard questions.* What do you wish you had done differently? Have you learned anything? If someone else had done this thing, would it change how you think of them?

- *Be brave.* If the door is still open to someone you may have affected, reach out! A message, a letter, even a small gesture to try to rebuild trust. If the door is closed, then I want you to write a letter of forgiveness to yourself. Make a promise to yourself that with this forgiveness comes a commitment to be better moving forward. Write out how you'll intentionally live that out today, tomorrow, and forever.

Your past beliefs, old dreams, and even your long-held regrets are not written in stone. You can edit your life as many times as you need—and want—to.

At the end of the day, the only thing worse than being wrong is refusing to grow when you finally realize the error of your ways. So go ahead and pick up that pen, cross out whatever no longer serves you, and write the next chapter of your life exactly the way you want it. Trust me, Bestie—it's going to be a bestseller.

“

Growth isn’t betrayal,
changing your mind
isn’t weakness,
and expanding your
worldview doesn’t
mean the old you was
a total f-ing idiot.

”

CHAPTER 19

DREAM SO BIG IT SCARES THEM

Hey, Bestie! You know that look people give you when you tell them your big dream? Like, the *big* dream. The one that often makes people respond with a slightly concerned, moderately amused, or even fully condescending head tilt. Or they might say something supportive, but you can still sense that underlying tone of, "Oh, sweetie. Are you sure about that?" That reaction right there—*that's* when you know you've stumbled onto something.

If you have what feels like a huge dream—a dream so big that it sometimes makes you feel delusional—and it doesn't make at least one person clutch their pearls, then maybe that dream is still too small. The best dreams, the ones that will change your life and maybe even the world, are the kind that make other people nervous. Not because they don't believe in you (well, okay, maybe some of them don't, but fuck those guys), but because your ambition reminds them of all the ways *they* have settled.

Once, at a dinner party, a man chuckled when I told him I was an influencer. That less-than-polite chuckle might as well have been a middle finger right in my face. It hurts and can be demoralizing when people react to your dreams and accomplishments in unkind or cavalier ways. But here's the thing I've come to understand: People will always laugh at or dismiss things they don't understand. They will scoff at dreams they're too afraid to chase. They will warn you of failure, not out of concern or wisdom, but because they can't stand watching you soar toward the sun when they chose to keep their feet firmly rooted on earth.

I still dream big. And I'm not talking about getting-a-few-more-brand-deals type of dreams. I'm talking big as in I want my own talk show. Like full-on cameras, couch, live audience, glam squad type of bitch. And every time I say that dream out loud, I watch the same expression wash over people's faces. It's like they are trying to hide their repulsion with a supportive smile. But the eyebrows always give it away. You can almost hear them thinking, *Riiiiiiiiiigggghhhht.*

But I say it anyway. All the time. Because I am someone who manifests the things I want. I don't just wish for them, I speak them into existence. I write in my journal just like I'm having you do, and I daydream about them on my music-less walks. I hold them to my chest. It's not about being delusional (although that helps), it's about being devoted to my vision, my path, myself really. I have no idea how or when or who will say yes, but I know in my bones that I'm going to have that show. I just am.

I used to shrink a little when someone would tilt their head to try to understand if they heard me correctly. I used to think that I was aiming too high. But the longer I've immersed myself in S.A.S.S., the more I have affirmed my worth. I've realized that other people's reactions aren't a reflection of my talent or potential. They're a mirror of their own limitations. That head tilt? That smirk? That's about them, not me. They're poor saps and their inner critics are dressed up as logic.

I've worked way too hard and come too far to limit my dreams to what makes other people comfortable. If anything, I hope my big, audacious dreams make people feel as uncomfortable as possible. But I also hope that my truth and my dreams shake something loose in them. Dreams are supposed to be a bit scary—that's how we know they're worth chasing.

One of my favorite "what if it all works out?" stories is about my friend Nick. I met Nick while I was performing at a dinner theatre in Colorado. He was a waiter, not an actor, serving the guests while they ate before the show. He was pretty quiet, but not shy. He had a great work ethic and was constantly moving, and always met people with kindness and a sly sense of humor. It was common for the waitstaff and the actors to mingle after the show at the bar. One night, Nick was rolling silverware while I wiped the stage makeup off my face. And like always, he was talking about desserts.

Not in a "I like cookies" kind of way, but in a "I tried putting orange zest in my shortbread recipe and that was just the extra oomph it needed!" kind of way. He clearly had a passion. But like so many people, he just filed that passion under "hobby" and kept working as a waiter. You know what I mean. The job that paid the bills but dimmed his personal light. Still, I loved talking to Nick about his desserts. Mostly because he would bring them into the theatre for us to try, and they were really good! But it was also nice to chat with someone who had such a spark for something.

Many years went by after my time at that theatre ended, and I eventually lost touch with Nick. We hadn't been super close, and our lives went in different directions. But one day in 2021 when the world collectively told COVID to go fuck itself and we were all in the process of rebuilding our lives, I saw a post from Nick on social media. It was a picture of him standing in front of a beat-up food truck. The caption read, "I'm really doing it! I quit my job and I'm starting my own food truck!"

The expression on his face was so funny because it looked like he just committed a crime but also won the lottery. I didn't tilt my head, nor did I smirk. Instead I commented, "AS YOU SHOULD!"

But not everyone was as affirming. I sent him a message asking how everything was going. He told me that he was so excited but that some of the people closest to him, including family, were trying to bring him back down to earth. They reminded him how unstable the food industry can be and thought he should go back to his old job and try the food truck thing as a side hustle. He expressed that he wished they would have believed in him, but he knew in his gut that he was doing the right thing.

The beginning of his new business seemed rough. He had sold his car just to be able to buy this secondhand truck. He posted about the stress of having to learn about plumbing and mechanics because he couldn't afford to pay someone else to fix the problems. He ended up picking up shifts at a restaurant in order to be able to afford supplies. But I just kept thinking of this peach cobbler he made that was so sweet and comforting it tasted like Southern charm wrapped in a hug. I really wanted it to work out for him.

A couple of weeks later he started posting about finally getting out there and starting to sell his stuff. I asked him again how it went, and he said, "I sold three cookies. Made nine dollars. I'm equally horrified and proud." I told him that one day he's going to make $900 in a day and to keep going.

And slowly, that day came.

It wasn't overnight. I remember seeing posts where he talked about the struggles of owning your own business and some months where you barely break even. One other time I saw him post a picture of his truck next to the porta-potties at a food truck court. Nothing screams "Try my peach cobbler" like a man exorcising a demon out of his ass 12 feet away from you.

But the momentum was there. His social media for the truck was growing, and he was getting write-ups in local publications. When he posted a one-year celebration story, he also introduced his first ever employee along with it. He was able to take one day off each week now, something he hadn't done in like a year and a half. And he seemed more grounded than I had ever seen him when he was waiting tables at that small dinner theatre in the Rocky Mountains.

On one of my posts celebrating my one millionth follower, Nick sent me a message to congratulate me. I returned the cheer and told him how cool it was to watch him absolutely be crushing it with his desserts. He said, "Thanks, man. You were one of the first people who didn't laugh at me." And that made me feel so good. It wasn't funny. It was brave.

I asked him what was next, and he told me he had bigger dreams to open up a brick-and-mortar location of his business and maybe even host baking classes there. How cool is that?

That's the thing about dreams so big that they scare people—the dreams don't stay still. They grow and evolve, just like your cute little ass is doing. Those dreams might ask more of you, but they're also willing to give more back. I watched Nick chase his dream, stumble a bit, but then get up and keep going.

Bestie, I want you to build a life where success doesn't feel like a single-file line of opportunities that run out if you don't grab them before someone else gets to them. There is room for you *and* for everyone else to chase down those ridiculous, jaw-dropping goals.

I want you to go after your biggest dreams loudly, shamelessly, and fearlessly. If people laugh, let them. If they doubt you, let them. If they're jealous, that's on them, not you. What others believe has nothing to do with your ability or your future. Dream so big it scares them. Dream so big it scares *you*. And then do it anyway.

Now that I've told you my dreams and shared how my friend Nick dared to believe in his own impossible dream, let's talk about you. Because I know there is a dream inside you right now. Maybe it's hard to know what it is because it's been under the weight of bills, work, kids, health shit, doubt, and a million other reasons that will tell you why now isn't the time. Or maybe that dream is already banging on the walls of your heart telling you to let it out already.

As your Bestie, I have to tell you that if you've ever shared that dream with someone and they made you feel like you need to tuck it away, you should have only one question for them: Why are you so consistently opposed to deodorant, you stinky bitch? But seriously, fuck them.

Now, if you are the one who rolled your own eyes at your own dream, I'll be more gentle and remind you of all the incredible things you've been learning about yourself so far, and I hope you can revisit that dream with a fresh new perspective of what you're capable of.

If your dream doesn't rattle a few people, maybe it isn't big enough. Dreams are supposed to wake us up, and that undoubtedly will make some folks uncomfortable. Remember, it just reminds them of their resistance to their own growth.

Let's uncover that big dream of yours, the one that might have been buried under "someday." I want you to start by writing down three big dreams you've had or currently have in your life. Don't censor yourself, no matter how impossible or silly these dreams sound. Just write them down.

Do any of them make your heart race a little? That's your little dream alarm going off! And now I want you to pick one small action you can take this week that supports that dream. Maybe it's signing up for a class. It can simply be telling someone you trust about your goal. Some things that I do are making a vision board or writing out a one-page outline of what my goal looks like. Pick an action and execute it, babe.

You don't have to launch an entire dream tomorrow. Remember my messy room analogy? The end result can be overwhelming and paralyze you from even starting. Just find a small actionable step and focus on that. I am telling you now that if you feel some discomfort here, it's largely because other people have made you believe you need to prioritize practicality over passion. But your dreams are valid, even this one.

Whether your dream is having your own talk show, a bakery, writing a damn self-help book, or running your own farm, it's not too late. Dream that dream that makes even you clutch your pearls.

“Build a life where success doesn’t feel like a single-file line of opportunities that run out if you don’t grab them before someone else gets to them.”

CHAPTER 20

THE BENCH WHERE BLESSINGS SIT

Hey, Bestie! As you know by this point, I love to express how I'm feeling by telling stories—and I've saved one of my favorites for this final leg of the journey. This is a story about a very special gift that's come as a result of this life I've built and the way I choose to engage with the world around me. Because that's the thing about sculpting your life and centering yourself as the main character in it: Beautiful things are always coming your way.

Yes, there are the headlines, like your lifestyle, your career, and your partner—but so many other gifts and experiences come from living your life out loud and in a way that's unwaveringly reflective of who you are and where you want to go.

One Sunday morning about two years ago, I woke up earlier than usual. I poured myself a cup of coffee and took care of the dogs, but my boyfriend (now-husband) was still asleep, so I decided to go for a run. I put on my sneakers, popped in my earbuds, and out the door I went.

A couple of miles into my run, I stopped to tie my sneaker at a bus stop. As I was bent over, minding my own business, I heard a voice ask, "Can I sit down here?" I looked up and saw an older woman, dressed up like she was going to the Kentucky Derby.

"Of course," I said, scooching over.

The woman introduced herself as Georgia. She told me she had just walked up the hill and needed to take a break to catch her breath. She was on her way to church, and while she loved church, she hated the walk to get there because it was difficult for her.

I listened intently as Georgia spoke because I know the feeling of needing a friend. Over the last few years, I've become intentional about talking with people when given the opportunity because you never know who else needs a friend too. I've always thought it strange that in modern times we have an endless amount of information at our fingertips, which *should* result in us being more interesting, but really, so many people live their life with their head buried in their phone. I've learned so much more from talking with people and understanding how they feel and why. Every chat with a stranger gifts me a little nugget of wisdom that I otherwise wouldn't have learned or considered, and that I can use to make me a fuller Misha.

I asked Georgia if she knew anyone else in the congregation who might be able to drive her to church. She explained that nobody from the church offered to help, even when she mentioned the treacherous walk, and she went on to tell me that she was a widow and all her children had moved away. As we continued talking, I learned that Georgia hadn't mentioned to any of her kids that she was struggling with these walks because she was afraid of losing her autonomy. She feared that if they found out, she would be forced out of the home she had created for herself and have to move into a different type of home where she would lose her independence.

I sat with Georgia for quite some time as she caught her breath and regained the strength to finish her walk. She asked what I did, and when I explained, she said she wanted to see some of my videos. Listen, I'm a millennial white gay guy and Georgia is a Black Southern octogenarian, so I'd be lying if I said I didn't feel some hesitation in showing her my videos, but she surprised me by laughing hard at some of them.

"Yeah, I have a mouth on me; it's not for everyone," I said a bit sheepishly as we both watched me cuss onscreen.

"Oh well. That lady yelling at that cashier deserved it." Georgia shrugged as she continued watching the video.

As we leaned over laughing together, I felt that spark that comes with those special, easy, and instant connections. I told Georgia that I would be happy to give her a ride to church and even attend with her anytime she wanted. We swapped phone numbers and went our separate ways.

I've learned something really powerful in the last few years of my life, and it is *that something* that only shows itself when you stop rushing through life and start living in it. That something is the little voice. You know the one. The curious tug that tells you to pause here, say hello, ask that question. It tells me constantly that people I meet might be important.

For so long I lived in fear of being forgotten and yet I felt totally alone. I realized that this little voice inside my head had always been there, but it wasn't as loud as those bitches Fear and Doubt. This voice was trying to gently nudge me in the direction of connection, and I just couldn't hear it. But after doing the work of loving myself, of quieting the chaos inside my head, I have been able to hear it more clearly. And more importantly, actually listen to it.

I don't mean that you need to be best friends with every person you meet at Target. But if you find yourself in a lingering conversation, and if something inside you feels pulled toward this person, don't brush it off. You never know the lesson, or even the laughs, that a woman in orthopedic shoes and a wide-brimmed hat can offer you.

I know that I probably missed out on a lot of beauty in the world because I was looking for the grand, flashy, obvious signs from people who I thought could fix me. I missed the everyday people that, like Georgia, who sat next to me to catch her breath, could have caught my heart.

The following Friday, I texted Georgia and told her that I had been serious about giving her a ride to church if she would like one. I have to admit that I, myself, would be a little apprehensive about getting in a car with a practical stranger, so I was a little surprised when she texted back: *That would be lovely. Thank you!* The next Sunday morning, I drove up to Georgia's apartment to pick up my new friend and off to church we went.

I didn't grow up going to church and could probably count the number of times I'd gone other than for a wedding on one hand. I was nervous and didn't really know what to expect when we pulled up to a small, unassuming white building across the street from a Whataburger. In the end, it was just a regular service and I had nothing to be worried about—but it felt special because it was the day that solidified my and Georgia's new and unlikely friendship.

Over the course of the next year, I accompanied Georgia to church more Sundays than not. We ruffled the feathers of a couple who didn't appreciate a gay guy coming into their church, but Georgia always backed me up and claimed my spot in the pew. One week I had to miss mass because I was out of town, and the man in this couple (who, by the way, looks like the scary old neighbor with a shovel in *Home Alone*) had the audacity to tell Georgia that hopefully I wasn't there because I *had died*! Georgia tattled on him to me like a sibling tattles to their parent, *knowing* he would get in trouble.

When I returned the next week, I walked up to him and I said, "Oh, hey! I heard you wished death upon me in the house of the Lord last week, just like a good Southern Baptist would do. I just wanted to let you know I'm here because I give Georgia a ride to church every week because walking here is painful for her. Something that none of you seemed to either notice or care enough to do anything about. So I'm here because you didn't love thy neighbor enough, bitch."

He responded by telling me that I looked like I didn't belong there. I told him that he looked like he was heading out west to pan for gold, and if God had given me a face that looked as weathered as his, I wouldn't be praying to Him—instead I'd be pissed. As Georgia took my arm and pulled me away, she told me that I was more Christ-like than this guy would ever be.

We walked out to my car and Georgia reached over and put her hand on my arm in the way only a mother knows how and said, "You know, baby, God doesn't make mistakes. You are not a mistake." And she wasn't just saying this because she's a sweet Southern lady, she meant it in her bones. It wasn't just her support that hit me like the holy spirit, it was her pride in me.

Georgia didn't just accept me, she celebrated our friendship. And as someone who spent years shrinking to fit into rooms that didn't want all of me, being seen and defended by this soft-spoken woman hit me right in the heart. You never forget the people who fight for you. And she did that not only by standing up to that couple, but by sitting next to me every Sunday. She didn't need to wave a rainbow flag to show me that she was on my side, her heart was big enough to recognize mine was enough.

At 83 years old, Georgia took the Internet by storm. My stories about her received tens of millions of views. The two of us could not be more different, yet here we were, building a friendship that proved we are all more alike than we are different.

Georgia didn't have any form of social media herself, and I think that's another reason why people loved her so much. She was so innocent, and in the alternately highly curated and dark place that is social media, she was a welcome change. For example, my first story about Georgia was a very simple retelling of how she asked me to take her to the library if it wouldn't be too much trouble because she'd read all the books she owned many times and wanted to dive into new stories.

I asked her if she'd ever thought about getting a Kindle so that she could literally have any book she desired at the touch of a button.

She said no, she had never considered such a thing. I decided to buy her one, and when I told the story online, I received thousands of comments from people offering book recommendations and letting Georgia know that she could get free books from the library on her Kindle. Something about her brought people together in a very community-driven way.

Thanks to social media, I also connected with Georgia's daughter. Georgia had told her about me, so when one of my videos about Georgia came across her daughter's feed, she put two and two together. She reached out to me via email, thanking me for looking out for her mom and saying how grateful she was to know someone was taking care of her.

Despite the fact that I was a system of support for her, Georgia's health became too difficult to manage on her own over the course of the next year, and it was decided she should go live with her daughter 2,000 miles away. On the last day that I got to spend with Georgia, we reflected on our time together, and I told her how lucky I was that all my recent life choices—taking the time to consider where my life was going, giving myself permission to change course (which brought me to Texas), and sculpting my life to one of service to others—were like a perfect storm that blew me over to landing on that bus stop bench at the exact moment Georgia arrived.

"And you should be proud of those choices," Georgia said, looking at me solemnly. "You have built this man in front of me brick by brick. And how lucky am I that I got to have you as a friend?" Before she left, Georgia gave me a pin that had belonged to her husband and told me that he would have loved me for loving her the way that I did.

A few months later, I got a call from Georgia's daughter letting me know that she had passed away peacefully, with her children by her side.

The thing about my friendship with this octogenarian woman I randomly met at a bus stop is that she taught me things I don't think many other people could have. She shared her faith in God with me, and I watched on as she embodied those beliefs in the way she lived. She was patient, charitable, and saw the good in everyone. By proxy, she taught me to form my own opinions of things rather than listening to what everyone else has to say.

Being gay, and now in Texas, I would have never walked into a church on my own, where the narrative is that I don't belong. That first Sunday morning, nervous about walking into a building where I worried I might burst into flames upon entering, she told me, "It's always the smallest group of people who are the loudest. But that doesn't mean they're right." And she was correct. That one couple made a big fuss about me being there, but they were the only ones. Every other member of the congregation appreciated what I was doing for Georgia. The whole experience expanded my ability to focus on the things that I can see with my own eyes, rather than on what others tell me.

And now, Bestie? It's your turn to go sit on your own bench and look around. Not waiting for someone to come and save you—you've done a hell of a job doing that yourself. You get to sit there and choose what comes next. Because when you live a life rooted in self-love, you start seeing the world differently. You catch the blessings that other people miss.

Every choice you've made to take care of yourself—every time you stood your ground, affirmed your worth, or rewrote your story—it's led you right here. And now you get to sculpt a life that makes space for even more connection and a lot more magic.

That's the real gift of doing all this hard work. When you start showing up, so does the universe. Sometimes it is in huge ways, like how my career completely shifted, and other times it's in a quiet moment on a bus stop bench. You haven't just changed your life, you've changed the way you're able to receive it.

So here is your final assignment, Bestie. This week I want you to find your own bench. Like actually sit on a bench, or find your metaphorical one, and just sit and breathe. I want you to think about the blessings you have in your life right now that you have only because of the choices that you've made. Let it sink in. How powerful is that?

But now I want you to ask yourself another question. If life can feel this good already, what else might be waiting for you just around the corner? I want you to keep up your intentionality and recognize the blessings that come your way this week and take the time to pay attention.

You've done the work. You've met yourself again. Now go take your place in the world, Bestie. Not in the back row, not on the sidelines, but front and center. Because the life that you're sculpting, it's not just possible . . . it's blessed.

“Because that’s the thing about sculpting your life and centering yourself as the main character in it: Beautiful things are always coming your way.”

CONCLUSION

Well, Bestie, here we are! It might be the end of the book, but this is just the beginning of your main character arc. I hope you are so proud of yourself for getting this far. If you're reading this, you've gone through some brutal self-reflection. *Ouch.* But so necessary. You've affirmed the bad bitch that you are, and you've stood your ground without apologizing for it. You are now in the process of sculpting a masterpiece—your life.

So congratulations! You're a full-blown sassy gay man. Kidding. You are becoming the person you've always dreamed of being. You've practically got a degree in being your own bestie. (Which is a lot more useful than a lot of other degrees. Trust me, I know; I went to school for musical theatre.) You have embraced your S.A.S.S.

I hope you've realized that you've done a lot more than just read some words on a page. You've shown up for yourself. That's huge. And I hope that you continue to show up for yourself every damn day moving forward. Even if you stumble, you can come back and take the lessons you've learned to course correct before you fall too far.

And what do you do now? You go *live.* You don't have to wait for someone to give you permission to take up space and sparkle as brightly as you desire because the world may never be ready for that, and that's okay.

Give yourself permission to rewrite your story, to change your mind, to be a work in progress, and, most importantly, to love yourself through it all. Continue to expand your dreams, what you expect out of life and of yourself, and the joy you allow to filter into your life.

I wasted so much time being worried about people who didn't bring me that joy—the Mateos, the Gabbys, and the Beas of the world. Shift your focus and instead cherish the Courtneys, the Jens, and the Georgias—the people whose presence feels like being hugged by Nana, who loves you so much.

Don't be afraid to stumble. I know how I used to feel when I messed up. Like I ruined everything and what was the point of trying to fix it? Bestie, the truth is that you will continue to mess up because that's just part of being human. But that doesn't mean you need to throw yourself or your progress in the trash like the romaine lettuce I buy every week to make salads but instead find brown and wilted in the back of the fridge come Friday.

No, we learn, we pivot, we keep it moving. This journey wasn't ever about becoming a flawless, perfectly polished version of yourself who never makes mistakes. No, being your own bestie means standing by yourself even when you feel like a hot-ass mess. It's looking in the mirror with your puffy eyes, when you are wondering, *What are you even doing, bitch?*, and still loving yourself.

My intent was never to help you create a new version of yourself. I just wanted to remind you of who you've been all along. You are in control. And if anybody, including that bitch-ass hater voice in your head, says otherwise? They can kindly see themselves out, thank you very much. Be fabulous, be fearless, be your own bestie.

Love ya!

ACKNOWLEDGMENTS

Big love to my dream team: Marc Gerald and Leah Petrakis at Europa Content for believing in this from day one, Lisa Cheng and Monica O'Connor at Hay House for turning my sass into an actual book, and my managers Philip Battiato and Chris Motyl for always pushing me to do one more thing.

To my book coach Nikki Van Noy, you gave me the tools and the confidence to actually use them. To my husband, Shane, thank you for cheering me on, pretending like my earlier drafts were hilarious, and not telling my editors that I don't actually know how to read or write.

And to all my Besties, online and off: You've sparked the joy and calling that made this book possible. Truly, this one's for you.

ABOUT THE AUTHOR

Misha Brown is an undeniable entertainment powerhouse, influencer, podcast host, and performer who shot to the spotlight on TikTok with the viral Lessons in Not Crossing a Gay Man series, amassing over 6 million followers. Named Motivational Creator of the Year and honored by the Webby Awards for social impact, he also earned a Best Comedy Podcast nomination from the Podcast Academy. Misha's work has been recognized by *People*, *USA Today*, and *Good Morning America*, cementing his status as one of the most compelling voices online.

@yourbestiemisha

Hay House Titles of Related Interest

YOU CAN HEAL YOUR LIFE, the movie,
starring Louise Hay & Friends
(available as an online streaming video)
www.hayhouse.com/louise-movie

THE SHIFT, the movie,
starring Dr. Wayne W. Dyer
(available as an online streaming video)
www.hayhouse.com/the-shift-movie

* * *

BECOMING FLAWESOME:
The Key to Living an Imperfectly Authentic Life,
by Kristina Mänd-Lakhiani

BRAVE NEW YOU:
A Road Map to Believing That More Is Possible,
by Cory Allen

PROTECT YOUR PEACE:
Nine Unapologetic Principles for Thriving in a Chaotic World,
by Trent Shelton

UNANXIOUS:
50 Simple Truths to Help Overthinkers Feel Less Stress and More Calm,
by Humble the Poet

YOU ARE MORE THAN YOU THINK YOU ARE:
Practical Enlightenment for Everyday Life,
by Kimberly Snyder

All of the above are available at your local bookstore,
or may be ordered by contacting Hay House (see next page).

* * *

We hope you enjoyed this Hay House book. If you'd like to receive our online catalog featuring additional information on Hay House books and products, or if you'd like to find out more about the Hay Foundation, please contact:

Hay House LLC, P.O. Box 5100, Carlsbad, CA 92018-5100
(760) 431-7695 or (800) 654-5126
www.hayhouse.com® • www.hayfoundation.org

Published in Australia by:
Hay House Australia Publishing Pty Ltd
18/36 Ralph St., Alexandria NSW 2015
Phone: +61 (02) 9669 4299
www.hayhouse.com.au

Published in the United Kingdom by:
Hay House UK Ltd
1st Floor, Crawford Corner,
91–93 Baker Street, London W1U 6QQ
Phone: +44 (0)20 3927 7290
www.hayhouse.co.uk

Published in India by:
Hay House Publishers (India) Pvt Ltd
Muskaan Complex, Plot No. 3,
B-2, Vasant Kunj, New Delhi 110 070
Phone: +91 11 41761620
www.hayhouse.co.in

HAY
HOUSE